Who is the 'Angel of the Lord'? Is it
Andrew Malone engages in a careful
'christophany' texts. He provides a tl
issues and offers some fresh thoughts about how the New Testament
interprets the Old Testament. A great work on the hermeneutics of
the so-called christophanies – well worth reading!
Michael Bird, Lecturer in Theology, Ridley College, Melbourne

Did God appear to ancient Israel? Who is the mysterious Angel of the
Lord who crops up throughout the Old Testament and seems to be very
much like God himself? In this engaging study, Andrew Malone takes
us through the various interpretations that have been given to this
phenomenon and explores their plausibility in the light of the biblical
evidence. His presentation is lively, making the book accessible to a
wide public, and his conclusions are underpinned by serious scholarship.
A must read.
Gerald Bray, Research Professor of Divinity, Beeson Divinity School

For many years I have commented in class that I want to do more work
on those mysterious references to the Angel of the Lord, on the fact
that some people saw God while other passages say he isn't seen, and on
how we are to think about the progressive revelation of the Father, Son,
and Spirit across the Bible's unfolding narrative. Andrew Malone has
done the work for us! Here is a careful sifting of the evidence, a close
reading of the texts, and a mature, cautious, logical, passionate, and
convincing treatment of these questions. You'll be glad you read this
engaging book.
*Jim Hamilton, Professor of Biblical Theology, The Southern Baptist Theological
Seminary*

Modern interpreters and preachers are often quick to identify the
appearance of the Angel of the Lord as a pre-incarnate appearance of
Christ. While Christ himself says that what we call the Old Testament
anticipated his coming (see Luke 24:25–27, 44–49), Andrew Malone
makes a persuasive argument that we should not identify the Angel as
a christophany. This accessible, well-written book is a must read for
everyone who wants to interpret the Bible correctly.
*Tremper Longman III, Robert H. Gundry Professor of Biblical Studies,
Westmont College*

KNOWING JESUS
IN THE
OLD
TESTAMENT?

KNOWING
JESUS
IN THE
OLD
TESTAMENT?

A FRESH LOOK AT
CHRISTOPHANIES

ANDREW MALONE

FOREWORD BY DAVID PETERSON

INTER-VARSITY PRESS
Norton Street, Nottingham NG7 3HR, England
Email: ivp@ivpbooks.com
Website: www.ivpbooks.com

First published 2015

British Library Cataloguing in Publication Data
A catalogue record for this book is available from the British Library.

ISBN: 978-1-78359-204-3

Set in Monotype Garamond 11/13pt
Typeset in Great Britain by CRB Associates, Potterhanworth, Lincolnshire
Printed and bound in Great Britain by Ashford Colour Press Ltd, Gosport, Hampshire

Inter-Varsity Press publishes Christian books that are true to the Bible and that communicate the gospel, develop discipleship and strengthen the church for its mission in the world.

Inter-Varsity Press is closely linked with the Universities and Colleges Christian Fellowship, a student movement connecting Christian Unions in universities and colleges throughout Great Britain, and a member movement of the International Fellowship of Evangelical Students. Website: www.uccf.org.uk.

CONTENTS

ACKNOWLEDGMENTS

All theology is formed in conversation with others. This book itself is intended to stimulate existing discussion, exegesis and theologizing further. So I am grateful to those who have participated so far: scholars and lay people both distant and near in time and space. I am especially thankful for a wife who saw swiftly the issues at stake in this topic, children who have tolerated my research throughout their lives, supervisors and colleagues and editors who have refined my thinking and writing, and friends and family who have shown interest in and prayed for my investigations. May we all progress in our shared quest to know, love and serve our triune God and his self-revelation in the Old and New Testaments better.

Give thanks to the LORD, for he is good;
his love endures for ever.
(Ps. 107:1)

Andrew Malone

FOREWORD

When Christians who believe in the inspiration and authority of the Bible disagree over significant matters of interpretation, it is often because deeper issues are at stake. Such is the case with the debate about whether appearances of God in the Old Testament were actually preincarnate manifestations of the Son of God, the second person of the Trinity.

In this searching study, Andrew Malone draws together some of his previous work on the topic and engages with a broad range of scholarly opinion, ancient and modern. But he does so with a preacher's passion to explain and illustrate key issues for the uninitiated. For example, most of us would not have spent much time reflecting on biblical statements about the invisibility of God. Why is this important? Most would not have been seriously concerned about the relationship of the Angel of the Lord to the Lord himself. Does this really matter? Few would have considered the exegetical implications for Old Testament interpretation of Jesus' claim that he existed before Abraham (John 8:56–58) or Paul's claim that Christ was with the Israelites in the wilderness (1 Cor. 10:1–4).

After a thorough examination of critical texts and different interpretative approaches, Andrew contends that there are no compelling reasons for specifically identifying Old Testament theophanies as appearances of the Son of God. This may be disappointing for some readers, but Andrew's concern is for us to be driven by the evidence of the texts themselves. Other agendas, such as the desire to show how God as Trinity engages with his people in the Old Testament, must not be allowed to distort our reading of the text.

Even if you are not troubled about whether the Son of God appeared to Old Testament characters before his incarnation, you will find this book a helpful challenge concerning the way to read Scripture. In particular, Andrew deals with the vital issue of interpreting the Old Testament in the light of God's ultimate self-revelation in the person and work of the Lord Jesus.

David Peterson

ABBREVIATIONS

AB	Anchor Bible
AGJU	Arbeiten zur Geschichte des antiken Judentums und des Urchristentums
ANF	*The Ante-Nicene Fathers: Translations of the Writings of the Fathers Down to A.D. 325*, ed. A. Roberts and J. Donaldson, 10 vols. (Peabody: Hendrickson, repr. 1994)
AOTC	Apollos Old Testament Commentary
AV/KJV	Authorized Version / King James Version
BBR	*Bulletin for Biblical Research*
BECNT	Baker Exegetical Commentary on the New Testament
Bib	*Biblica*
BNTC	Black's New Testament Commentaries
BSac	*Bibliotheca sacra*
BST	The Bible Speaks Today
BT	*Bible Translator*
CBQ	*Catholic Biblical Quarterly*
CEV	Contemporary English Version
Chm	*Churchman*
CSEL	Corpus scriptorum ecclesiasticorum latinorum
CTQ	*Concordia Theological Quarterly*
DBSJ	*Detroit Baptist Seminary Journal*

DDD	*Dictionary of Deities and Demons in the Bible*, ed. K. van der Toorn, B. Becking and P. W. van der Horst, 2nd ed. (Leiden: Brill; Grand Rapids: Eerdmans, 1999)
DOTP	T. D. Alexander and D. W. Baker (eds.), *Dictionary of the Old Testament: Pentateuch* (Downers Grove: InterVarsity Press, 2003)
EBC	*The Expositor's Bible Commentary*, ed. Tremper Longman III and David E. Garland, rev. ed., 13 vols. (Grand Rapids: Zondervan, 2006–12)
EGGNT	Exegetical Guide to the Greek New Testament
Enc	*Encounter*
ESV	English Standard Version
EvQ	*Evangelical Quarterly*
GNB	Good News Bible
HCSB	Holman Christian Standard Bible
HSM	Harvard Semitic Monographs
IBC	Interpretation: A Bible Commentary for Teaching and Preaching
IVPNTC	InterVarsity Press New Testament Commentary
JETS	*Journal of the Evangelical Theological Society*
JSOTSup	Journal for the Study of the Old Testament: Supplement Series
LCC	Library of Christian Classics
NA²⁸	Nestle-Aland *Novum Testamentum Graece*, ed. Barbara and Kurt Aland, Johannes Karavidopoulos, Carlo M. Martini and Bruce M. Metzger, 28th rev. ed. (Stuttgart: Deutsche Bibelgesellschaft, 2012)
NAB	New American Bible
NAC	New American Commentary
NASB	New American Standard Bible
NCB	New Century Bible
NCV	New Century Version
NDT	*New Dictionary of Theology*, ed. Sinclair B. Ferguson and David F. Wright (Leicester: Inter-Varsity Press; Downers Grove: InterVarsity Press, 1988)
NET	NET Bible: New English Translation
NICNT	New International Commentary on the New Testament

NICOT	New International Commentary on the Old Testament
NIGTC	New International Greek Testament Commentary
NIrV	New International Reader's Version
NIV	New International Version
NIVAC	NIV Application Commentary
NKJV	New King James Version
NLT	New Living Translation
NRSV	New Revised Standard Version
NT	New Testament
NTS	*New Testament Studies*
OT	Old Testament
PL	Patrologiae, cursus completus, patres ecclesiae, series latina, ed. J.-P. Migne, 221 vols. (Paris: Cerf, 1844–64)
PNTC	Pillar New Testament Commentary
ResQ	*Restoration Quarterly*
RTR	*Reformed Theological Review*
SPCK	Society for the Propagation of Christian Knowledge
TNTC	Tyndale New Testament Commentaries
TOTC	Tyndale Old Testament Commentaries
tr.	translation, translated by
TynB	*Tyndale Bulletin*
VTSup	Vetus Testamentum Supplements
WBC	Word Biblical Commentary
WTJ	*Westminster Theological Journal*
ZNW	*Zeitschrift für die neutestamentliche Wissenschaft und die Kunde der älteren Kirche*

1. GETTING ORIENTED

'Michael Bird is wrong!' There's a sentence I never thought I'd utter.

Some people don't know or care who Michael Bird is and how he performs.

Those of us who know Mike should be a little more cautious about challenging him. Especially when he's a prolific young scholar who has penned a dozen significant theological tomes (and also a novel). Especially when he edits books, journals and commentaries, and runs a well-subscribed blog (with influential book reviews). Especially when he is jetted off to important international speaking engagements (and hangs around for pleasure with the likes of N. T. Wright). And especially when he has recently been appointed as a teaching colleague (and is, I hope, party to a growing friendship)!

Apart from his international academic standing I'm hesitant to challenge Mike, because he's a nice guy who's about as orthodox as they come. He is committed to understanding and living out and teaching others the Scriptures. He is keen to defend the historical Jesus and the writings of Paul. He wants to shape the church and its doctrine and practice around our triune God. As he expressed once at a staff gathering, he is a Christian whose every move is a response to 'the utter worshippability of Jesus Christ'.

But even orthodox people can make mistakes.

What is a christophany?

Mike scores mention here because of his approach to Old Testament christophanies. He is part of a growing trend that believes and teaches that God the Son, the second person of the divine Trinity, made tangible appearances before becoming incarnate as Jesus of Nazareth. Bible readers are encouraged to spot Jesus walking and talking in the Old Testament. That's how the word 'christophany' is employed these days, especially in conservative circles where Jesus and the Old Testament are highly valued.

It's all the rage to investigate a hero's backstory. The *Star Wars* trilogy was so successful that George Lucas made another three episodes introducing Darth Vader. We've been subjected to *Young Indiana Jones*, *Batman Begins*, and any number of prequels to Superman, Spider-Man, the X-Men, Sherlock Holmes, the *Star Trek* universe, *The Wizard of Oz* – and any other franchise that's not yet been wrung dry. Christophanies scratch a similar itch. They offer potential insights into the backstory of Jesus, long before we traditionally meet him one silent night in the little town of Bethlehem.

The idea of Jesus' Old Testament cameos has existed throughout church history. Justin Martyr was a philosopher who became an ardent apologist for the faith. Writing almost exactly a century after Jesus' incarnate earthly ministry, Justin colourfully insisted that 'Anyone with even half a brain would not dare suggest that the Maker and Father of everything left all the things of heaven and beyond and appeared on a small patch of the earth.'[1] With God the Father sequestered in heaven, Justin argued that appearances of God in the Old Testament were appearances of God the Son, glimpses of the preincarnate Christ.

---

1. Justin Martyr, *Dialogue with Trypho* 60.2. While the idiomatic translation here is mine, the exaggerated sentiment is Justin's.

That's what 'christophany' means, though the word itself is relatively new. The word is composed from two Greek terms that together mean 'an appearing of Christ'. In many scholarly works, the word describes appearances of Jesus after his resurrection. Whether or not we know the word, readers of the Gospels and Acts are familiar with the christophanies of Jesus to Mary Magdalene at the tomb, to the two mourners on the Emmaus road and to various gatherings of disciples in Jerusalem (Luke 24; John 20; Acts 1). Perhaps the most famous is the christophany to Paul on the Damascus road (Acts 9). Paul also catalogues numerous other New Testament christophanies as he verifies the hundreds of eye-witnesses to Jesus' resurrection (1 Cor. 15:3–8).

Old Testament christophanies?

This book is concerned with the possibility of christophanies prior to Jesus' resurrection and prior even to his incarnation. That's how the word is increasingly used in conservative circles. It's even possible that the word 'christophanies' is now applied more to Jesus' Old Testament appearances than to his New Testament ones.

The Old Testament application is appropriate, because that's the very context that brought us the word. German and French studies of Justin Martyr in the 1840s analysed his interest in christophanies, and the *Oxford English Dictionary* judges that the English equivalent was spawned in 1846. The word can then be found in a number of theological writings in the latter half of the nineteenth century on both sides of the Atlantic. However, it then seemed to languish somewhat, employed only occasionally through the first three quarters of the twentieth century.

This application, however, has some specialized nuances. To investigate these nuances we need another related word, 'theophany', which means 'an appearing of God'. Most readers are familiar with the many Old Testament theophanies, when God appeared to Abraham at various points in his life, to Moses in the burning bush on Mount Sinai, to the Israelites rescued from Egypt and gathered at that same mountain, to various kings and prophets, and so on. Some of these are said to occur in dreams, but for the most part they're presented as everyday encounters between God and people. Of course there's nothing common about being confronted by God, but the Old Testament employs everyday words to describe God's 'appearing to' or 'coming to' or 'speaking with' humans.

In orthodox Christianity, Jesus is God. So everyone accepts that the words 'christophany' and 'theophany' are related. The question at stake is how they're related. There are at least three possible combinations. These aren't mutually exclusive, but they invite us to consider more thoughtfully what's being claimed.

1. No Christian doubts that every appearance of Jesus is a way of seeing God. Jesus himself assured his disciples, 'Anyone who has seen me has seen the Father' (John 14:9). Every christophany is a kind of theophany.

2. God's actions in the Old Testament are often considered to be executed by all three members of the Trinity together. On those occasions it's safe to allow that every theophany *includes* a christophany. (Each theophany also includes what scholars might call a 'pneumatophany': an appearing of the Spirit.)

3. As we'll see, the resurgent trend is to argue that Old Testament appearances of God are appearances of the Son alone. The Father and the Spirit are not involved in these manifestations to humans. The two technical terms take on a different relationship; we are supposed to interpret every theophany specifically or exclusively *as* a christophany. When 'God' appears to Abraham and Moses and others, readers familiar with the New Testament are invited to interpret this more narrowly as 'God the Son' appearing to Abraham and Moses and others.

This third, exclusive, sense is under scrutiny here. No conservative Christian doubts Jesus' post-resurrection materializations. But an increasing number now reserve the word to emphasize his preincarnate appearances in the Old Testament. This is what Justin himself proclaimed and how the term 'christophany' was applied to his writings.

The resurgence of Old Testament christophanies

It seems both the word and the concept have been returned to prominence by theologian James Borland. The title of his 1976 doctoral dissertation clearly spells out his thesis: 'Christophanies: Old Testament Appearances of Christ in Human Form'. A popular- ization appeared in 1978, with sufficient interest that a second edition was released in 1999 (itself reprinted and freshly promoted in 2010). Borland focuses on the human-form theophanies and chooses the word 'christophanies' as his shorthand annotation. Theologically, he understands the word in the third sense above. Christophanies are

> the exclusive function of God the Son . . . Christ alone appeared in the human-form theophanies . . . solely the second person of the Godhead . . . Christ was the sole agent of the Christophanies . . . none other than the second person of the Trinity – God the Son.[2]

Old Testament scholar Walter Kaiser Jr. wrote the foreword to Borland's book, echoing Borland's lament over the limited interest in Old Testament Christology. Although perhaps occasionally more circumspect in his exegesis and application, since then Kaiser has championed both the word and several of the attendant issues. His prolific publications and his connections with major theo- logical institutions and societies have given 'christophanies' a global hearing.

The impetus offered by Borland and Kaiser coincided with the word starting to regain currency in other theological writings. The volume on *Exodus* in the popular Tyndale Commentary series used the word in 1973. So too a 1975 article in the *Zondervan Pictorial Encyclopedia of the Bible*. Encyclopedias, journal articles and study Bibles of the 1980s and 1990s progressively picked up the term. Some were merely descriptive and were not endorsing the narrower under- standing of theophanies. Yet the increased frequency of the term has convinced subsequent authors that the word is common and the phenomenon accepted. It's also possible to find the phenomenon enthusiastically endorsed even if the word is not employed.

---

2. James A. Borland, *Christ in the Old Testament: Old Testament Appearances of Christ in Human Form*, 2nd ed. (Fearn: Mentor, 1999); here pp. 58, 59, 60, 62, 63.

Consequently, 'christophanies' are now named in a veritable swathe of twenty-first-century writings. The term is found in academic dictionaries, commentaries and journal articles on biblical books as diverse as Genesis, Exodus, Daniel, John and Hebrews. Although it's still sometimes used of New Testament, post-resurrection appearances, it is now substantially applied to Old Testament theophanies and in the narrow, exclusive sense. It's found especially in popular and conservative presentations and further cemented by influential preacher-authors such as Chuck Swindoll, R. C. Sproul and Mark Driscoll. Under the normative subtitle *What Christians Should Believe*, the latter assures us that 'the Old Testament teaches about Jesus through appearances that he makes before his birth, or what are called *Christophanies*'.[3] While such teaching is concentrated in more conservative congregationalist contexts, the word and concept can be found in the technical writings of high-church Anglican and Roman Catholic scholars and the concept at least in Lutheran and Presbyterian studies.

Comments like Driscoll's give the impression that christophanies are an academic *fait accompli* with no further ratification required. My colleague Mike Bird likewise assumes the notion is a given and promulgates the sensation that christophanies have been established by rigorous scholarship. Mike's freshly minted textbook lists the latest reprint of Borland's work for further reading and endorses his interpretation. 'Another approach to finding Jesus in the Old Testament asserts that certain theophanies (appearances of God) in the Old Testament were in fact christophanies (appearances of the preincarnate Jesus).' Indeed, even though Mike mentions New Testament christophanies as well, his index and definitions focus exclusively on the Old Testament occurrences.[4] Mike's tome is from

---

3. Mark Driscoll and Gerry Breshears, *Doctrine: What Christians Should Believe* (Wheaton: Crossway, 2010), pp. 44–45.

4. Michael F. Bird, *Evangelical Theology: A Biblical and Systematic Introduction* (Grand Rapids: Zondervan, 2013), p. 360. Old Testament applications and definitions are given (pp. 103, 360–361), while the New Testament sense goes undefined and unindexed (pp. 716, 774).

a leading Christian publisher; it is titled an *Evangelical* summary and intended to be an authoritative textbook for future generations of theological thinkers and leaders; it focuses on God's trinitarian revelation of himself through both testaments of Scripture; and it sold out and a second printing was commissioned within weeks of release. It seems certain to cement Old Testament 'christophanies' further in the vocabulary and interpretative practices of conservative Bible readers.

Investigating christophanies

Despite what prominent authors such as Kaiser, Driscoll and Bird might intone or imply, there's not really a lot of academic rigour poured into this area of scholarship. The idea of Old Testament christophanies sounds so plausible, yet there's much less actual evidence once we start poking and prodding. Its popularity is like a pious urban legend: a few Christians have heard the suggestion somewhere and successive others have amplified it. Everyone believes it primarily because the person before believed it. Our task throughout this book is to suspend the rumour chain and probe the claims a little further for ourselves. Like good detectives we want to move beyond plausible-sounding innuendo and assumptions and circumstantial evidence.

Good detectives are aware of their own biases. So it's helpful for us to consider our own motivations and how these will influence our approach to the evidence and its interpretation.

Having already surveyed much of the evidence myself, I'm aware that I'm advocating a great deal of caution on the topic. I don't think the usual evidence and arguments really stack up. Readers will have to gauge how fairly and completely I introduce and evaluate the case for christophanies.

I'm also aware of the temptation to pick out a straw opponent. It's simple (and sometimes satisfying) to caricature a position and its proponents inaccurately or unkindly so as to highlight its failings and promote an alternative. As we'll see shortly, a lot can ride on one's interpretation of christophanies, and the conversation has not always been cordial.[5] I'm picking out Mike Bird precisely because he is the antithesis of straw; he is flesh and blood and in my face each working week. He is no academic lightweight, and his passion for orthodoxy, for our triune God and particularly for this God's self-revelation through Jesus and through the Bible cannot be doubted.

So I'm writing for people like him. People who love Jesus and the Bible. People who want to maximize the value of the Old and New Testaments as God's vehicle for revealing more about himself. I dare not consider this to be the final word on the subject. Rather, it is intended to be a repository of some of the thinking that has been achieved to date and to be a catalyst for further, careful consideration of the possibility that Jesus made distinct appearances to humanity prior to his incarnation in the opening pages of the New Testament. I offer it as a charitable stimulus to orthodox believers such as Mike who want to hone further their use of the Scriptures and their adoration of our majestic, revealing, triune God.

You may be ready to race ahead to the next chapter and see how things play out; that's fine. The rest of this introductory chapter offers a little more background to the issues involved, why they are attractive, and what aspects of biblical interpretation they have an impact on.

Not everyone shares the same evangelical values that Mike and I do. Even then, he and I differ over the topic of christophanies. You yourself may be reading this book from one of several possible viewpoints. It can be helpful to consider your own orientation before exploring the topic.

You may not have heard of christophanies before. I hope you will get a reasonable introduction to the phenomenon, to the reasons it is sometimes held in high regard, and to some of the interpretative issues under consideration.

You may well be reading this book because you are a Christian believer who finds the idea of christophanies influential. If so, you

---

5. Reviewers in *JETS* of both of Borland's editions mention his 'pejorative language' and 'dismissive or derogatory terms' concerning those who don't share his views (William J. Larkin Jr., *JETS* 23 [1980], p. 163; Ray Lubeck, *JETS* 44 [2001], p. 332).

are part of a dignified Christian heritage that stretches back at least to the second century. Please recognize that, even where we differ on the interpretation, we are all motivated by the same goal: to better understand God and how he has revealed himself in every part of Scripture. As we work through the arguments that have so far been raised in favour of this phenomenon, we'll find plenty of orthodox interpreters who've preferred different ways to understand the evidence. One's views about christophanies have sometimes been invoked as a litmus test of orthodoxy, but I think that's outrageous. Godly, Bible-believing Christians have always been found on both sides of the fence. It's an internal disagreement, not one that rules some people 'in' and others 'unsaveable'!

If you're especially persuaded by the idea and keen to share it with others, I invite you to work through the cautions I raise. We certainly share the commission to bring the story of Jesus to the wider world as effectively as possible, which includes a commitment to incorporate the Old Testament in the first and future steps of Christian believers. Yet I wonder if promoting christophanies can be unhelpful for both the believers and unbelievers in our care. For those who don't believe the gospel, I'm uncertain that promoting christophanies will prove convincing. In fact I worry that enthusiasm for christophanies can present as more of an in-house, self-congratulatory kind of exercise – and one whose circular logic and unsubstantiated academic foundations may alienate those who are still learning about Jesus (or perhaps later embitter some who discover this initial selling point to be infirm). For those who come or continue to believe, I'm concerned that we should not teach unproven theological assumptions or irresponsible methods of reading the Bible. In both making and maintaining followers of Jesus, Old Testament christophanies may not be the firmest theological foundation we can offer.

It may be that, as you read this, you are not particularly fond of Jesus or the Old Testament. I hope you will hear the careful distinctions I'm trying to draw. Just because I'm unconvinced by the arguments in favour of Jesus as the sole participant in Old Testament theophanies does not mean that Jesus was never active in the Old Testament or that he never existed at all. Nor am I suggesting that the Old Testament holds no value for Christian readers or for

Christian theology. Just because one small set of arguments proves
to be incomplete and unconvincing does not invalidate many of the
wider ends towards which such arguments are employed.[6]

Regardless of your own stance it remains true that a good
number of conservative Christians, past and present, have striven
to demonstrate Jesus as visibly active in the Old Testament. Even
as I query the veracity of christophanies, I trust you'll find that I'm
still a big fan of Jesus and of the Old Testament. We'll even find
plenty of evidence for his eternal existence and his work prior
to the New Testament. I just don't think christophanies are a
responsible or conclusive way of verifying these. To the contrary,
I think the notion can damage Christian growth. It can teach us to
read the Scriptures poorly. And it can also inadvertently paint God
the Father in quite a negative light: a recluse who's unwilling or
unable to interact with his world. That's one legacy of Justin Martyr
we don't need to inherit.

You should also find positive corollaries to these cautions I
raise. As we investigate what the Bible is not saying about christophanies and theophanies, we should expect to learn better what
it does say. As we query whether it is God the Son exclusively at
work in Old Testament appearances, we should expect to appreciate more about God the Father. Contrary to Justin, I think there
are many reasons to *affirm* that the Father (along with the Son and
the Spirit) has always been ready, willing and able to participate
in the world he created.

The attractions of christophanies

Apart from correct doctrines of God the Father and God the

---

6. There are various more careful works, such as Christopher J. H.
   Wright, *Knowing Jesus Through the Old Testament* (London: Marshall
   Pickering, 1992), against whose title my own plays, and Sidney
   Greidanus, *Preaching Christ from the Old Testament* (Grand Rapids:
   Eerdmans, 1999). Mike Bird helpfully includes these works among
   his suggestions for further reading.

Son, quite a lot of theological and practical value can be placed upon the possibility of christophanies. Let's consider some of the leading reasons why they are sometimes upheld as a central truth.[7]

Making sense of the Old Testament

The simplest attraction is that christophanies make the Old Testament much more obviously a Christian document. It is worth considering just how valuable christophanies are in this respect.

Approaching the Old Testament can be taxing. Sure, it includes some memorable highlights, some famous names and a plethora of moral lessons and dress-up dramas ready for children's programmes. But it often feels like a tedious introduction through which we must trudge before, more than three quarters of the way through the Bible, the story of salvation advances in earnest at the first Christmas.

The value of the Old Testament has been increasingly rediscovered in many Christian circles over the last few decades. It has been made more accessible to Christian readers, especially through the renewal of interest in biblical theology. Readers now have a big-picture framework within which to understand the earlier stories and their messages (as well as the more familiar contributions about Jesus and the church). We can trace God's grace as he chooses a nation for himself, through whom all the families of the earth will be blessed. We catch glimpses of the significance of creative power, of sin-cleansing sacrifices, of tabernacles and temples, of priests and kings, of miracles, of wisdom and justice and righteousness, of praise and hope and resurrection. We're thus better equipped to appreciate how all these arcs eventually meld in exquisite

---

7. Some of the following are pondered by Borland, *Christ in the Old Testament*, pp. 101–117; Andy Saville, 'Paul Blackham: A Trinitarian Reading of the Old Testament', *Chm* 123 (2009), pp. 341–360; 'The Old Testament Is Explicitly Christian', *Chm* 127 (2013), pp. 9–28; Andrew S. Malone, 'Paul Blackham (Parts 1&2)', *Chm* 125 (2011), pp. 51–71, 151–172.

combination in the person and work of Jesus Christ, God the Son incarnate.[8]

How much more appealing is this lengthy 'introduction' if Jesus himself made guest cameos!

Making the Old Testament palatable is a hard task in some churches. Finding Jesus there would mean preachers and study leaders don't have to work so hard at showing the relevance of the first thirty-nine books of the Bible. We would be less likely merely to moralize or to risk questionable allegorical parallels or to abandon altogether these three quarters of Scripture. It positively invites us to consider why God has devoted so much space in the Christian Bible to this 'prequel'. It can rejuvenate our preaching and reading plans and encourage Old Testament content for adults' and children's programmes alike. It gives leaders and laity permission to move beyond a steady diet of a favourite Gospel and preferred letters of Paul. Paul affirms that all Scripture is inspired by God, and the prospect of discovering Jesus may be just the catalyst needed to put this doctrine into practice and to venture into these often murky and unexplored depths.

Making sense of the New Testament

Finding Jesus in the Old Testament actually enhances our appreciation for the New Testament as well.

Orthodox Christians have always affirmed that God the Son is eternal, existing right back to (and even before) the creation of the universe. His incarnation at the first Christmas was a hugely significant step in his interaction with creation, but it wasn't the beginning of his existence or activity. John's Gospel begins with the affirmation 'In the beginning was the Word', through whom all things were made

---

8. Among various such works, one popular 'rediscovery' of the whole-Bible story is offered by Vaughan Roberts, *God's Big Picture: Tracing the Storyline of the Bible*, rev. ed. (Nottingham: Inter-Varsity Press, 2009). A recent focus on Jesus' centrality in such arcs is David Murray, *Jesus on Every Page: 10 Simple Ways to Seek and Find Christ in the Old Testament* (Nashville: Thomas Nelson, 2013).

(John 1:1–3). Other New Testament authors sustain these tenets (e.g. 1 Cor. 8:6; Col. 1:15–17; Heb. 1:1–3), which are echoed in many of our creeds and songs.

Actual evidence of Jesus' activity in the Old Testament aids our appreciation for such passages. It also helps with other New Testament texts. Jesus himself identifies the Old Testament as relevant to his ministry, suffering and resurrection (Luke 24:25–27, 44–47; John 5:39, 46). His apostles further reinforce this as the New Testament progresses (e.g. Acts 10:43; 26:22–23; 1 Pet. 1:10–12) and quote the Old Testament to this effect (e.g. Acts 2:22–36; Heb. 1:5–13). Some New Testament passages even seem to locate Jesus physically in Old Testament events (esp. John 8:56; 12:41; 1 Cor. 10:4, 9; Jude 5).

Protecting theological orthodoxy

Christophany proponents note some further theological incentives. If we can identify God the Son (and God the Spirit) as active in the Old Testament, we can more readily avoid the mistake of thinking that God was once one and became three only later in the story. Or we'll be less likely to slip into various heresies that Jesus was merely human and was somehow adopted by God or infused with deity after a regular, creaturely conception. We'll certainly be armed against cynical secular assumptions that the Judeo-Christian world view evolved at the whim of successive human inventors, with the Old and New Testaments contradicting each other on matters such as God's triune nature.

Cultivating theological interest

Modern marketing gurus know how to repackage overly familiar content. Our favourite films and television series are rereleased in newer formats with bonus features. We're especially partial to previously unseen material. Likewise, anticipating the expiry of fifty-year copyright protection, artists such as the Beatles and Bob Dylan are formally releasing some of their alternate recordings from the 1960s. Avid fans of either medium can be captivated by even the smallest variations from what they're used to.

Finding Jesus in the Old Testament is similar. Variations on the usual melody can be refreshing. And there's the enticement of chancing upon some snippets that have been previously disregarded or altogether unpublished.[9]

We ought not to underestimate sensations such as discovery. For those unacquainted with christophanies, there's the exhilarating thrill of unearthing something previously unknown. Upon recognition that the concept (though not the word) has been in circulation since the first generations of Christians, there's a dignified sense of antiquity and authenticity in reconnecting with those ancient interpreters. A modern generation of sceptics trained in the vein of *The Da Vinci Code* may even wonder if this important interpretative insight was somehow suppressed for centuries by church authorities. Innovation, nostalgia and conspiracy are each highly prized in contemporary Western culture.

Creating evangelistic entrées

It is not only Christian readers who stand to benefit from discovering Jesus among the pages of the Old Testament. It is exciting to think that members of other cultural and religious contexts may enjoy a new avenue for meeting Jesus.

People with Jewish or Muslim sympathies are often hesitant to approach the New Testament, but many are open to (and sometimes firmly in favour of) the writings of Moses and the prophets. Knowing how to discover and demonstrate the triune God from the Old Testament is an attractive evangelistic option. It offers an avenue to Jesus along which fewer prefabricated roadblocks have been erected.

Where are we going?

Discovering Jesus more patently in the Old Testament is a winning scenario by any Christian measure. But, as the revived proverb intones, with great power comes great responsibility (cf. Luke 12:48). To the extent that we want to build such practical, pastoral, theological and evangelistic edifices upon the prospect of christophanies, we want to be sure of the foundations.

---

9. Murray, *Jesus on Every Page*, pp. 73–74.

Again, there's yet to be a convincing presentation of the case for christophanies. It's not at all clear that this ultimate jackpot can be claimed with the confidence sometimes expressed. In the coming chapters we'll investigate the major arguments that keep surfacing. Some of these appear superficially to be quite solid, but the promising veneer does not bear further scrutiny. The circumstantial evidence is, indeed, circumstantial. Other arguments are valid in certain other contexts, but not in this particular context.

In short, we want to be better Bible readers. That's precisely what proponents tell us is achieved when we interpret theophanies as christophanies: we are clarifying the trinitarian truths inherent in Old Testament passages. I propose that we can become even more responsible in reading and interpreting the Bible by *challenging* the arguments used for christophanies. We share the same quest, we just differ on how to interpret the evidence. My role in the investigation is to suggest, perhaps naggingly, that we do not settle for superficial interpretations. We need to scrutinize the evidence ever more closely rather than hastily pronounce the case closed as soon as we think we have nailed our preferred suspect.[10]

The following chapters investigate three of the primary arguments upon which claims of christophanies are founded. These include the assumptions that God the Father must be invisible, that the Old Testament 'Angel of the Lord' must be God the Son, and that the New Testament concretely establishes Jesus' activity in Old Testament times. There *is* merit in each of these considerations – but not to the extent that we should too confidently construct claims about the person and work of Jesus being visible in Old Testament passages. Even though it may feel at the 'expense' of stealing the spotlight away from God the Son, we'll find ways to honour the Trinity better and more accurately read the Scriptures that our triune God has inspired for our life and doctrine.

---

10. Those uncertain about the foundational steps in biblical interpretation might explore popular introductions such as Nigel Beynon and Andrew Sach, *Dig Deeper: Tools to Unearth the Bible's Treasure*, repr. (Nottingham: Inter-Varsity Press, 2010), or Gordon D. Fee and Douglas Stuart, *How to Read the Bible for All Its Worth*, 3rd ed. (Grand Rapids: Zondervan, 2003).

PART 1

IS GOD THE FATHER INVISIBLE?

2. SEEING GOD IN THE OLD TESTAMENT: YES!

Admiral Piett raced down from the bridge of the star destroyer *Executor*, determined to voice his concerns personally to Darth Vader. Arriving unannounced, Piett found himself confronted with a sighting of the dark lord's unhelmeted head.

Viewers of all ages had waited breathlessly for this second movie of the original *Star Wars* trilogy and its barest glimpse of Vader unmasked. On screen, Admiral Piett pondered if he had overstepped some boundary and put himself in danger of joining several predecessors, themselves now breathless, who had offended this arch villain.

Years before anyone had heard the name 'Anakin Skywalker' we were already fascinated with what lay behind the mask. We were beginning to discover that the face of the hero's father – though rarely seen and risky to sight directly – was not permanently hidden from view.

The foundational christophany argument

Of course it's risky to use Darth Vader to illustrate the good God who created, sustains and redeems the real galaxy. But there are a number of important parallels, and these parallels can aid us in thinking about one of the foundational reasons why Old Testament theophanies are sometimes said to be christophanies.

Perhaps the most substantial rationale offered for christophanies boils down to a single assumption: that God the Father is permanently invisible to human eyes. The primary argument for christophanies incorporates this premise into a traditional three-stage syllogism:

1. Old Testament figures are said to have seen God, but
2. God the Father is invisible, therefore
3. Old Testament figures saw the Son, not the Father.

The logic really does sound rather convincing. No wonder it has been echoed throughout church history. It was a major element in Justin Martyr's presentation, which was then reprised over the next few centuries by the famous church fathers Irenaeus, Tertullian, Origen and Eusebius. For the first three hundred years after Jesus' death and resurrection there are references to the idea of the Father's invisibility – and thus to the Son's starring role in Old Testament theophanies. The overall argument is still marshalled by popular and scholarly authors who find merit in the notion of christophanies.

The syllogism is not actually complete. In particular it does not explain why it must be God the Son who makes appearances on behalf of the Trinity. Why not the Spirit instead of (or as well as) the Son? The overt claim about the Father's invisibility is usually supplemented by the orthodox assumption that the Son rehearses that role in Old Testament theophanies. We can find this approach articulated by some of the famous Reformers, such as Calvin.[1]

---

1. These chapters are developed from my article 'The Invisibility of God: A Survey of a Misunderstood Phenomenon', *EvQ* 79 (2007), pp. 311–329. Keen readers will find there some of the historical and scholarly references.

Checking the premises

In asking whether it's the Son or the Spirit who makes appearances, we've already raced ahead. We've already bought the assumption that the Father is not involved in visible theophanies. We've started to pass judgment without adequately reviewing the evidence.

Although the evidence sounds plausible and is widely touted, closer scrutiny suggests that it is not this simple. Throughout part 1 we discover conflicting interpretations. The Old Testament clearly presents God as appearing to and being seen by humans. Yet the New Testament sounds equally adamant that God cannot be seen. Proposing the Son's involvement is a plausible and attractive resolution of this tension. Other plausible resolutions exist but are not often investigated. As we review the evidence we'll find that the word 'invisible' probably does not mean what we think it means. There are thus better explanations of the Old and New Testament passages, explanations that don't require christophanies. We become better Bible readers without having to see Jesus in the Old Testament.

God makes himself seen

The first premise in the syllogism is not the contentious one. The issue of christophanies surfaces only because everyone recognizes the Old Testament's frequent mention of God's being seen. The question of who is visible wouldn't arise if the Old Testament didn't regularly recount that 'God appeared to Abraham.'

But the Old Testament is rife with such blunt language. The current chapter considers this language, giving us a sense of the problem that christophanies supposedly solve. It need not detain us long, because everyone agrees there are many occasions when God is said to be encountered in some kind of tangible fashion.

Like many languages, Hebrew uses a number of different words to describe the act of seeing. Just one of these verbs, written as *r'h* (or *rā'āh* or *rā'â*), gives us enough to work with. It is universally accepted that theophanies are commonly narrated with forms of this verb, which is almost always translated as '(God) appeared to' or '(God) was seen by'. The list of theophanies becomes very impressive very quickly. God 'appeared' to each of Abraham, Isaac, Jacob, Moses, Joshua and David, and perhaps also to Samuel and Jeremiah. It is said that each of Hagar, Jacob, Samson's parents, Micaiah, Isaiah and Amos 'saw' God.[2]

And those are just the individuals. Similar language is used of larger groups. The most important of these is a ceremony at Mount Sinai when God formally constituted Israel as a nation. After Moses, Aaron and seventy-two elders ascended the mountain, we're told – twice – that they 'saw God' (Exod. 24:9–11). There are other possible theophanies to large groups, though these are less certain. We don't lose anything if we're unsure about them, but if they prove convincing we massively escalate the number of witnesses. When Aaron and his sons are ordained as the first priests, all the Israelites are told to purify themselves because 'today the LORD will appear to you' (Lev. 9:4). The end of that chapter confirms – twice – that God's glory appeared to and was seen by 'all the people' (9:23–24). It is possible that God's 'glory' is somehow different to God himself, but christophany proponents usually see them as interchangeable, as does Leviticus. We might even add the pilgrimages expected of all Jewish males three times each year (e.g. Deut. 16:16; 31:11). Although English Bibles translate the purpose as being for the men 'to appear before the LORD your God', many scholars read the Hebrew to say that these Israelites came '*to see* the face of the LORD your God'. Other passages might echo such group sightings, though the recipients of God's appearings are not specified (1 Sam. 3:21; 2 Sam. 22:11; Ps. 42:2).

Thus this one verb is regularly accepted as the primary way that Hebrew authors narrate Old Testament theophanies.[3] Even more importantly, these encounters are consistently understood to be at

---

2. You can explore encounters for 'appeared' in Gen. 12:7; 17:1; 18:1; 26:2, 24; 48:3; Exod. 3:16; 4:1, 5; Deut. 31:15; 2 Chr. 3:1; 1 Sam. 3:21; Jer. 31:3; and for 'saw' in Gen. 16:13; 32:30; Judg. 13:22; 1 Kgs 22:19 = 2 Chr. 18:18; Isa. 6:1, 5; Amos 9:1.

3. E.g. Jeffrey J. Niehaus, *God at Sinai: Covenant and Theophany in the Bible and Ancient Near East* (Carlisle: Paternoster, 1995), pp. 17–20; George W. Savran, *Encountering the Divine: Theophany in Biblical Narrative*, JSOTSup 420 (Edinburgh: T & T Clark International, 2005), pp. 49, 98.

God's behest. Conservative Bible scholars readily translate this verb as 'God made himself to be seen' or God 'showed himself'.[4]

Of course, it's possible that 'seeing' God does not really mean using one's eyes. In various languages, 'to see' can mean something like 'comprehend' or 'experience'. That is true for the biblical languages too, including this Hebrew verb. If we decide that all occurrences are metaphorical, we've changed the rules of the game; we've discounted the opening premise of the syllogism; we can stop investigating visual appearances of God. But most scholars, especially those who favour christophanies, readily accept that most (if not all) of the relevant passages *are* talking something that happens with human eyes and visual perception. As Paul's argument for the resurrection implies, dreams or hallucinations hardly explain appearances consistently witnessed by many individuals in sequence, and especially not when experienced simultaneously by the members of several groups (1 Cor. 15:3–8).

And that's just one verb! If we add more verbs we find God encountering even more Old Testament individuals and groups. God 'comes' to Balaam, Samuel and all his people. Israelites and others 'meet' God, and he them. Further verbs of sighting, moving and meeting exist.[5]

Put simply, the Old Testament freely and unashamedly applies to God the same verbs used of human sensation and motion. God comes and goes; he encounters people; he sees and is seen.

A key text

Of all the Old Testament passages that describe seeing God, Exodus 33:20 is regularly emphasized. What's especially important is that it's

---

4. Here, Eugene H. Merrill, *Everlasting Dominion* (Nashville: B & H, 2006), p. 77; Victor P. Hamilton, *Exodus* (Grand Rapids: Baker Academic, 2011), p. 43.

5. For 'come', see respectively Num. 22:9, 20; 1 Sam. 3:10; Exod. 20:20; Deut. 33:2; Pss 24:7; 50:3; 98:9; Isa. 3:14; 59:20; Mal. 3:1–2; for 'meet', try Exod. 3:18; 5:3; 19:17; Num. 23:3–4, 15–16.

invoked both by those who insist that God is strictly invisible and by those who are more comfortable with his making visible appearances. Which interpretation is correct?

Moses has returned up Mount Sinai to plead for the Israelites who stand condemned because of the golden calf incident. The narrator reminds us that Moses regularly enjoys a special intimacy with God: 'The LORD would speak to Moses face to face, as one speaks to a friend' (Exod. 33:11). Today, apart from forgiveness for their heinous idolatry, Moses pleads for assurance that God will continue accompanying his people as they escape from slavery in Egypt towards the Promised Land. Among such assurances, Moses requests, 'show me your glory' (33:18). Although God promises to confirm his goodness (33:19), he adds a significant and famous qualification: 'But you cannot see my face, for no one may see me and live' (33:20). This statement becomes crucial in understanding Old and New Testament passages about seeing God. It is all the more significant because this principle is regularly assumed but never explicitly articulated anywhere else in Scripture. Let us consider several implications.

First, we should note that the prohibition of 33:20 is precisely that: a prohibition. Moses is not told that he is physically *unable* to look upon God; he is not *permitted* to do so. Almost every major English Bible translates this ambiguously: 'you *cannot* see my face'. There are two reasons we should interpret this as describing what is permitted for Moses rather than what is possible. (1) God gives Moses a rationale: 'for no one may see me and live'. This implies that someone *can* succeed in seeing him, albeit with fatal consequences. This is an odd warning if God is imperceptible to human sight. (2) God immediately makes arrangements whereby Moses does see something of God's divinity (33:21–23). Indeed, Exodus proceeds to talk unashamedly of Moses being with and speaking with Yahweh – an encounter sufficiently intimate to alter Moses' visible appearance (e.g. 34:1–9, 27–35).

Secondly, we must consider what we mean when we talk about God's 'glory'. That's what Moses asked to see. God responds that it's fatal to see his 'face'. How do these terms intersect? It's easy to think God is using the terms interchangeably: denying Moses a glimpse of his face denies a glimpse of his glory. That's consistent with other occasions where God's 'glory' cannot be endured, even by Moses (e.g. 40:34–35; 1 Kgs 8:10–11; Ezek. 1:28). But this itself suggests that something *can* be experienced. There are many other passages where God's 'glory' is manifest, often in the sight of all Israel.[6] So we cannot automatically assume that God's glory is unseeable. Exodus 33:20 does not disallow God's ability to render himself visible; it merely reinforces that he can make himself *too* visible for human survival.

Thirdly, we should ask what it means that God's 'face' (or 'glory') is unseeable. The word 'face' is difficult to pin down. While it can refer to the front half of a human head, it typically means someone's line of sight or their presence. The context makes it clear that here it refers to God's presence, his very self. Indeed, this is the way that simpler translations render 33:14–15 (e.g. NLT, CEV, NCV, NIrV).

The combination of '(not) seeing' and 'face/presence' finds a helpful parallel earlier in Exodus. Tired of the plagues that God has brought through Moses, the Egyptian Pharaoh banishes Moses: 'Get away from me; take care never to see my face again, for on the day you see my face you shall die' (10:28 ESV). Moses is banned from seeing Pharaoh's face, but that hardly renders Pharaoh or his face invisible! Both 10:28 and 33:20 seem to be warning against the consequences of a *successful* sighting.

Again, as noted above, it's possible that this language of seeing refers to something more than laying eyes on someone. God may be saying here something more about experiencing God. Certainly, the language of 'seeing the face' of a ruler is formulaic for entering his presence.[7] So it's possible that Exodus 33:20 is doing more than prohibiting Moses from keeping his eyes open as God passes by. If so, then no one should be using this verse to claim in any way that God is physically unseeable.

Finally, it's significant that by the centuries around the New Testament, Jewish interpreters had failed to develop a view of God

---

6. E.g. Exod. 16:7, 10; Lev. 9:6, 23; Num. 16:19, 42; 20:6; Deut. 5:24; Ps. 63:2.

7. E.g. Gen. 43:3, 5; 44:23, 26; Exod. 10:28–29; 2 Sam. 3:13; 14:24, 28, 32; 2 Kgs 25:19; Esth. 1:14; Job 33:26; Ps. 42:2; Jer. 52:25.

as strictly invisible. Rather, various passages continue to aspire to seeing his 'face' and 'form' even during human life.[8]

Exodus 33:20 thus joins the consistent testimony of the Old Testament that God can be seen by human eyes. It's a question of whether God makes himself available for viewing and whether it's wise to do so.

Tripping up

Even before we consider other passages, it's helpful to observe how people's doctrinal assumptions can trip them up. As we'll contemplate later, our theological frameworks regularly influence our Bible reading. This is no less an issue when it comes to Exodus 33:20 and convictions about God's invisibility. Readers who assume that God is strictly invisible to human eyes can make a mess of verses like this one. We're offered a salutary lesson that some assumptions, including those that underlie christophanies, can actually impair our reading of Scripture.

We've already witnessed the prominence of James Borland and Walter Kaiser concerning christophanies. Each has also written commentary notes on the entire book of Exodus. Their commitment to God's invisibility makes their interpretations of 33:20 awkward. Borland generally allows that something of God was seen here, yet he also lists this among 'verses which declare the invisibility of God'.[9] Kaiser likewise judges this verse to be '[f]oremost' among 'passages that appear to argue that it is impossible to see God'. He conflates the two meanings of 'cannot', so that what is not permitted for Moses is then used as evidence for what is not possible for

---

8. E.g. Pss 11:7; 17:15; 140:13. For more of the relevant Jewish evidence, see Craig S. Keener, *The Gospel of John* (Peabody: Hendrickson, 2003), pp. 247–250, 423; Savran, *Encountering the Divine*, pp. 103, 206.

9. James A. Borland, *Christ in the Old Testament*, 2nd ed. (Fearn: Mentor, 1999), p. 99; cf. pp. 92–94; 'Exodus', in Edward E. Hindson and Woodrow Michael Kroll (eds.), *The KJV Bible Commentary* (Nashville: Thomas Nelson, 1994), pp. 178–179.

anyone. This attempt to hold two meanings simultaneously is even less sensible when the two effectively make opposite claims about whether God can be visible to human eyes.[10]

Other scholars, whether discussing this passage or others, can stumble similarly. We'll see more examples in coming pages.

Further Old Testament evidence

When we look beyond our key verb (*r'h*) and key verse (Exod. 33:20), we find the same principle consistently assumed throughout the Old Testament. God can be seen, albeit with the threat of fatal consequences.

We certainly find that many intimate theophanies are accompanied by a note of surprise that the humans who have sighted God have not perished instantaneously. On at least four occasions either the human witness or the narrator remarks on this survival. Clearly, the assumption is that God *can* be seen; although such sightings weren't everyday occurrences, it's not their viability that attracts attention. This is recognized by modern interpreters who carefully weigh the emphases of these stories: 'The issue is always a matter of life for the human beings involved, not God's visibility.'[11]

We'll take a moment to skim through the examples, because they're relevant to my discussion of the Angel of the Lord in part 2. Each account typically reinforces three main points: (1) everyday Israelites thought it possible to encounter the God of Israel, even to the point of seeing him in some kind of physical fashion; (2) they expected to incur death for doing so; but (3) such a penalty was not always exacted.

Genesis 16 introduces Hagar, the maid of Abraham's wife, Sarah. Hagar suffers from Sarah's erratic responses to her own barrenness.

---

10. Walter C. Kaiser Jr. (with others), *Hard Sayings of the Bible* (Downers Grove: InterVarsity Press, 1996), pp. 154–156 (quote on p. 155); cf. p. 152; 'Exodus', in *EBC*, vol. 1, p. 546.

11. Terence E. Fretheim, *Exodus*, IBC (Louisville: Westminster John Knox, 1991), p. 300.

Hoping to procure God's promised descendants for Abraham, Sarah gives Hagar to Abraham as a surrogate. The plan succeeds so well that Sarah regrets her decision and banishes Hagar. After encountering the Angel of the Lord, Hagar identifies 'the God who sees me' (16:13). The Hebrew wording is a little unclear here and different Bibles consider various interpretations. Several go so far as to describe Hagar as marvelling that she has '*remained alive* after seeing him' (e.g. NRSV, NASB). Such a translation is probably more speculative than necessary, but at the least it illustrates the persistent theme in Scripture that seeing God is possible, even if it is expected to be fatal.

In Genesis 32 Jacob wrestles with 'a man' by the Jabbok River. Everyone, including later biblical retellings of the event, recognizes this mystery man as God (cf. Hos. 12:3–5). Surviving the encounter, Jacob names the place 'face of God'. He gives the reason as 'because I saw God face to face' (Gen. 32:30). He then adds, 'and yet my life was spared'.

We have already observed how seventy-four Israelite elders ascended Mount Sinai and encountered God. The text is not only adamant that they saw God but also that – apparently to everyone's surprise – 'God did not raise his hand against these leaders of the Israelites' (Exod. 24:11). The narrator does not want his readers to miss or mistake this unexpected outcome. He repeats again that 'they saw God' but that, rather than dropping dead, they ate and drank safely in his presence: a sign of welcome.

The last major example takes even greater space to record the survivors' surprise. Judges 13 recounts the Angel of the Lord visiting Samson's parents on several occasions to announce the pending birth of their infamous son. The narrator lets readers in on the story, so we know it is the Angel at work. But Manoah and his wife merely think they are meeting 'a man of God' (though an impressive one); the narrator reassures us that Manoah is blind to his true identity (13:16). It is only after their final dramatic encounter that Manoah twigs. He expresses both his horrific realization and the expected consequence: '"We are doomed to die!" he said to his wife. "We have seen God!"' (13:22). This foreshadows my discussion of the Angel and overlooks several other elements in the story. But Manoah's dread is sufficient on its own to confirm that everyday Israelites had no doubt it was possible to encounter the living God.

There are several minor examples that may be mentioned in passing, all of which reinforce the same three observations. Each of Gideon, Isaiah and Ezekiel encounters a visible form of God (or the Angel of the Lord). Each of them responds fearfully because of this very act of seeing God (Judg. 6:22; Isa. 6:5; Ezek. 1:28). Each survives.

Such scenarios repeat throughout the Old Testament. When the high priest enters the Most Holy Place once each year, the elaborate instructions of Leviticus 16 explain how he can avoid the death incurred by inadvertently gazing on God (esp. 16:2, 13). When the Israelites first gather at Mount Sinai, Moses warns them not to attempt 'to see the LORD', which would prove fatal (Exod. 19:21). This reflects Moses' own earlier response: when God called from the burning bush, Moses had hidden his face lest he *succeed* in seeing God (3:6). That God might successfully be seen is also the reason often presumed for Elijah's covering his face in God's presence (1 Kgs 19:13) as do the seraphim in God's throne room (Isa. 6:2).

In short, the Old Testament knows nothing of an invisible God. As one scholar wrote nearly a century ago, *'The thought of the invisibility of God in the strict sense is in no way an Old Testament one . . .* In the OT the notion is pervasive that humanity *can* see God with human eyes.'[12] Yes, seeing God can be a dangerous venture; we'll witness some unhappy examples later. Yes, he often hides himself, not least for humans' safety. But many narratives suggest that God himself can arrange theophanies such that any unwitting participants are not automatically vaporized.

---

12. Rudolf Bultmann, 'Untersuchungen zum Joannesevangelium. Part B: Θεὸν οὐδεὶς ἑώρακεν πώποτε (Joh 1,18)', *ZNW* 29 (1930), pp. 177–178 (my tr.; italics original).

3. SEEING GOD IN THE NEW TESTAMENT: NO?

Only when we reach the New Testament do we read that visual encounters with God are supposedly impossible. Old Testament christophanies are the solution to a New Testament conundrum.

Some readers don't expect coherence between the myriad documents that make up the Bible, so there's no problem perceived if the Old and New Testaments present contradictory evidence. For those of us who think the Bible presents a more consistent message about an eternally consistent God, there are various solutions to the apparent differences concerning God's invisibility. We turn now from the Old Testament to consider what the New Testament contributes, before exploring a whole-Bible perspective in chapter 4.

We'll scrutinize three major issues concerning New Testament evidence. First, we discover just how pervasive the idea is that God the Father is utterly invisible. Secondly, we investigate how the biblical word 'invisible' should best be understood. Thirdly, we revisit the main New Testament passages and reconsider what they're emphasizing. The results suggest it's highly unlikely that we should be using this English word 'invisible' to describe the God who made and manipulates matter for his own purposes. Contrary to popular perception and presentation, the New Testament is not at odds with the Old Testament accounts of God's making himself visible to people. There's no dilemma that requires christophanies as the solution. Rather, we should rejoice at the prospect that God can be seen throughout the whole Bible.

The popularity of God's invisibility

Often celebrating Jesus as the tangible representation of God, familiar New Testament passages mention God's usual inaccessibility: 'No one has ever seen God' (John 1:18; 1 John 4:12); 'The Son is the image of the invisible God' (Col. 1:15); 'Now to the King eternal, immortal, invisible, the only God . . . whom no one has seen or can see' (1 Tim. 1:17; 6:16). Their familiarity makes the argument sound incontrovertible. Few blink when the second premise in the syllogism is expressed: God the Father is invisible.

We cannot underestimate how pervasive this thought is. It influences important commentaries: those books that students and preachers reach for to understand Bible passages better. Each author and commentary series mentioned here is highly prized in conservative evangelical circles; these opinions have travelled widely and been read deferentially.

> The words 'no-one has ever seen God' remind us of the invisibility of God, an important theme in the Fourth Gospel (cf. 5:37; 6:46) . . . Moses did not see God – only Jesus has seen God . . . It is a truism in both OT and NT, and certainly in the Fourth Gospel (1:18; 6:46), that no-one has ever seen God . . . It is a fundamental teaching of the OT that no human being has seen God . . . Moses never saw God.[1]

Others who explain John's Gospel similarly affirm 'an utterly indisputable principle' that God 'is invisible to physical eyesight'.[2]

---

1. Colin G. Kruse, *The Gospel According to John*, TNTC 4 (Leicester: Inter-Varsity Press, 2003), pp. 73, 157, 173.
2. Respectively, Gerald L. Borchert, *John 1–11*, NAC 25A (Nashville: B & H, 1996), p. 124; F. F. Bruce, *The Gospel of John* (Grand Rapids: Eerdmans, 1983), p. 44.

These New Testament commentators not only tell us about John and Jesus but also pontificate on Old Testament doctrine. Their comments leave little room for the Old Testament sightings we've already observed.

The same verdict is pronounced for Paul. To understand Colossians 1:15 we're assured that

> [In the Son] the invisible has become visible. Both Old and New Testaments make it plain that 'no one has ever seen God' . . . (John 1:18).[3]

> According to both the Old Testament and Judaism, as John puts it, 'no one has ever seen God' (1:18); he is, as Paul puts it here, *invisible (aoratos)*.[4]

We return to this term 'invisible' (*aoratos*) shortly. But again we see reputable commentaries on New Testament passages giving every impression that God's invisibility extends back into the Old Testament. Students and preachers who start with these popular New Testament verses – and everyone they nurture – will be yearning for an explanation of the Old Testament theophanies. How could God appear to so many people if God is never seen?

Notice the chain of dependence. The 'invisible God' of Colossians 1:15 is explained by appeal to John 1:18. In turn, when the adjective 'invisible' appears in an obscure phrase in Hebrews 11:27, commentators reference Colossians for explanation. Whether intentionally or inadvertently, influential scholars again reinforce that the Old Testament itself teaches what these New Testament passages suggest about God and his imperceptibility.[5]

It is no surprise, then, to find even Old Testament commentaries working hard to interpret the Old Testament claims of God's appearances. In Leviticus 16:2 God promises that, every year on the

---

3. Peter T. O'Brien, *Colossians, Philemon*, WBC 44 (Waco: Word, 1982), p. 43.

4. Douglas J. Moo, *The Letters to the Colossians and to Philemon*, PNTC (Grand Rapids: Eerdmans, 2008), pp. 117–118.

5. E.g. Donald Guthrie, *The Letter to the Hebrews*, TNTC 15, rev. ed. (Leicester: Inter-Varsity Press, 1983), p. 241; Peter T. O'Brien, *The Letter to the Hebrews*, PNTC (Grand Rapids: Eerdmans, 2010), p. 434.

Day of Atonement, 'I will appear in the cloud over the atonement cover' of the ark of the covenant. This is why that chapter gives the high priest such detailed protective instructions on how to enter the Most Holy Place where the ark is concealed. The Hebrew term translated '*in* the cloud' is flexible, but one commentator ignores all the usual options and the very wording of the verse to deny a visible appearance at all: 'It does not mean that the Lord is visible.'[6] Especially concerning the ark, the phrase 'the invisible Yahweh' proliferates in many influential Old Testament introductions, studies, commentaries and dictionaries.[7] We thus too easily fail to flinch when a prominent Old Testament scholar affirms, 'the Bible stresses that Yahweh is completely *invisible*, unavailable to human sight'.[8]

The pervasive insistence that God is utterly invisible drives even respectable scholars to challenge the persistent theophanies throughout the Old Testament. This is not to suggest that every scholar is wrong or that those quoted here are consistently mistaken (when given more space, they occasionally temper the stronger claims I have cited). Yet it's obvious just how much some cultural and philosophical traditions have influenced conservative biblical scholarship. In turn we can appreciate why the primary argument favouring christophanies is so readily accepted. No wonder believers and authors at more popular levels think scholars have God's invisibility – and thus christophanies – all sewn up.

The meaning of 'invisible'

Scholars may sometimes intend 'invisible' in a nuanced fashion. But the word is no longer adequate as a convenient shorthand. It

---

6. Nobuyoshi Kiuchi, *Leviticus*, AOTC 3 (Nottingham: Apollos, 2007), p. 295.
7. E.g. see the following NIVAC volumes: Robert L. Hubbard, *Joshua* (Grand Rapids: Zondervan, 2009), pp. 162–166; Bill T. Arnold, *1 & 2 Samuel* (Grand Rapids: Zondervan, 2003), p. 94, n. 7; August H. Konkel, *1 & 2 Kings* (Grand Rapids: Zondervan, 2006), p. 637.
8. Hubbard, *Joshua*, p. 165 (italics original).

is now too easily misunderstood and any nuance overlooked. We need to reconsider what we understand when encountering this word – and what the biblical authors themselves intended us to understand.

Our goal is to arbitrate accurately the apparent disagreement between the two testaments. The general trend is to take the New Testament passages as definitive and literal and to 'explain away' the Old Testament wording. Christophanies are proposed to rationalize the Old Testament theophanies that the New Testament insists cannot occur.

But what if the Old Testament passages are granted the more definitive and literal status? Can we 'explain away' the New Testament statements? Although it is the road less travelled, this approach turns out to be quite plausible. It starts with reassessing what 'invisible' means in the Bible.

As the Old Testament drew to a close, Greek thought increasingly flourished. Philosophers such as Plato (428–347 BC) and Aristotle (384–322 BC) probed the visible and invisible realms. Plato especially was fond of describing divinity negatively: God should be unlike anything in the imperfect created order. If creation is 'visible', by definition God must be 'in-visible'. And so a new Greek term was birthed. The adjective for 'visible', *oratos* (itself only recent; sometimes written *horatos*), yielded *a-oratos*. It's *aoratos* that occurs in key New Testament passages (Col. 1:15; 1 Tim. 1:17; Heb. 11:27) and that has cemented the notion of 'invisible' in Christian language.

Before considering such passages, it is instructive to consider how other Greek authors of the era understood and used the word.

Josephus' life overlapped with Jesus' disciples' (AD 37–100). Josephus uses *aoratos* to depict things that '*are* not seen' more than things that strictly '*can*not be seen'. At least five of his seven uses mean this. He describes the off-limits interior of the Jewish temple, a city concealed in the mountains, a cave at the bottom of a well, and the deep valleys around the fortress mesa of Masada. Only once does he describe something intrinsically invisible, the human soul, which 'remains invisible to human eyes, just as God himself'. This application, including mention of God, is important. But the other uses show that *aoratos* confirms only *that* something is unseen; it does not explain *why* the object cannot be viewed.[9]

This same sense is attested by another contemporary author, Plutarch (AD 46–120). Souls and divine forces are 'invisible', especially when he echoes forebears such as Plato and Aristotle. Yet Plutarch also uses the word for tangible items hidden from view. He writes of captive women who have been cloistered from men, 'incommunicado and invisible to others'. He describes war catapults and signal fires strategically stationed to be 'invisible to the enemies'.[10] The Greek word *aoratos* has this broader sense, and the English translation 'invisible' may be too narrow or misunderstood.

Scholars who delve into the origins and applications of the word confirm this broader sense. One wide-ranging study of theophanies summarizes it this way: 'In Classical Greek invisibility is normally affected [*sic*] by materially obstructing visibility'; it's not at all a statement about (in)tangibility. A standard Greek dictionary likewise promulgates this breadth of meaning: 'unseen, not to be seen, invisible'.[11]

This is further affirmed by similar negated adjectives in the New Testament. Preaching in Athens, Paul mentions an altar dedicated 'TO AN UNKNOWN GOD' (Acts 17:23). Paul means 'a god *not currently* known' rather than one forever unknowable. Jesus fences with the Pharisees about people eating with 'unwashed hands' (Matt. 15:20). He obviously means hands that '*have not* been washed' rather than those that '*cannot* be washed' (cf. Mark 7:2, esp. NRSV). The general consensus, backed by Paul's own explanation, is that the 'inexpressible

---

9. Respectively, Josephus, *Jewish War* 1.7.6 §152 (*Antiquities* 14.4.4 §71); 3.7.7 §160; 3.8.1 §341; 7.8.3 §280; 7.8.7 §346.

10. Respectively, Plutarch, *Alexander* 21.3; *Marcellus* 15.5; *Romulus* 29.5 (my tr.).

11. Respectively, W. Wesley Williams, '*Tajallī wa-Ru'ya*: A Study of Anthropomorphic Theophany and *Visio Dei* in the Hebrew Bible, the Qur'ān and Early Sunnī Islam' (PhD diss., University of Michigan, 2008), pp. 30–34 (quote on p. 31); Henry George Liddell and Robert Scott, *An Intermediate Greek–English Lexicon* (Oxford: Clarendon, 1889), p. 86.

words' he heard in a heavenly vision are not cleared for publication (2 Cor. 12:4, esp. NRSV, ESV); it's less likely he is describing concepts for which there is no adequate language. A similar phrase occurs elsewhere as Paul describes the Spirit's interceding through 'unspoken groanings' (Rom. 8:26 HCSB); though less consensus exists here, many scholars again affirm that the Spirit could (but does not) articulate his intercessions.[12]

In short, there's every basis to take such negated adjectives as describing something that, for whatever reason, does not happen. There is no claim being made as to whether it *could* happen or not. This means it's far wiser to translate the word *aoratos* as something that is currently 'unseen', not something that is permanently 'invisible'.

Biblical passages

We reach the biblical uses of the term. These reinforce what we've already discovered: it's better to describe God as (usually) 'unseen' rather than (always) 'invisible'. Of course, a concept – whether invisibility or christophanies – can be described without using a specific word, so we'll also consider other passages that describe God's not being seen. Space precludes an exhaustive analysis of every text; we'll sample the most significant ones and merely hint at how the conclusions apply to others.

The Greek translation of the Old Testament introduces *aoratos* three times. Two are inconclusive (Gen. 1:2; 2 Maccabees 9:5). But Isaiah 45:3 confirms our observations. God announces he is going to bring King Cyrus of Persia to rescue the Israelites from exile in Babylon. Cyrus is promised 'hidden treasures', 'concealed, invisible (*aoratos*) riches' (my tr.). No intangible spiritual rewards here, just regular earthly booty not currently on display to other marauders.

---

12. These references and sentiments from Markus Barth and Helmut Blanke, *Colossians*, tr. Astrid B. Beck, AB 34B (New York: Doubleday, 1994), pp. 195–196; Peter T. O'Brien, 'Romans 8:26, 27: A Revolutionary Approach to Prayer?', *RTR* 46 (1987), p. 70.

The New Testament does use *aoratos* of invisible, intangible things (Rom. 1:20; Col. 1:16). But those uses are applied to 'things'. The other three uses are applied to God. These affirm that God is usually 'unseen' – but that is different to saying he is 'incapable of being seen'.

Verbs of seeing

It should be no surprise that relevant New Testament passages discuss acts of seeing. After all, that is the whole point of exploring theophanies and christophanies: 'appearances' that were seen.

It's useful to pause and recognize that 'to see' bears a wide range of meanings. Along with physical sight, the English 'see' readily refers to various senses such as 'recognize', 'understand', 'experience', 'meet', 'visit' and even 'court'. I've used many such sight-oriented idioms throughout this chapter. So too with the biblical languages. Genesis records many of the theophanies where God is 'seen'. Yet the author is equally comfortable speaking of Pharaoh's 'seeing' the contents of his dream (41:22). Joseph 'sees' the *absence* of Benjamin (44:31). Blind Isaac exclaims, 'See, the *smell* of my son' (27:27, my tr.; cf. ESV, NASB). Later prophets are said to 'see' their oracles, even when these oracles come as much in words as in visions (Amos 1:1; Hab. 1:1).

We need to keep our eyes open to these varied uses. New Testament passages that appear to speak of not seeing God may be trying to say something slightly different.

John 1:18 ≈ 1 John 4:12

These two, nearly identical verses can be studied together. Scholars widely recognize they correspond to each other, both almost universally translated, 'No one has ever seen God.'

It's a pretty strong sentiment. We've already seen John 1:18 on high rotation when it comes to explaining God's invisibility; most other passages are dependent on this verse. Christophanies are all but demanded when the full verse reads, 'No one has ever seen God, but the one and only Son, who is himself God and is in closest relationship with the Father, has made him known.' The terms are strong ones. In Greek as in English, John sounds like the extreme claims we're used to from modern advertising: No one. Ever.

Period. What is John saying if he is not promoting God's absolute invisibility?

For a start, John is talking about more than physical sight. Within 1:18 he contrasts 'seeing' with 'making known'. The point is even more transparent when we observe 14:9. Using exactly the same verb, Jesus affirms that 'The one who has seen Me *has seen* the Father' (HCSB; cf. 12:45). Unless the verses contradict, we have to work out how God is seen according to 14:9 yet never seen according to 1:18.

The earliest interpreters recognized that the obvious solution is to allow that 'seeing' God means different things in different verses. Either or both means something like 'to understand' or 'to comprehend'. Our confidence in this interpretation increases by looking at how John uses such verbs. Where 14:9 affirms that seeing the Son is tantamount to *seeing* the Father, just two verses earlier 14:7 uses similar structure about *knowing* each of them: 'If you had known me, you would have known my Father also' (ESV). This hints that 'seeing' in John 14 may have more to do with comprehension. The two ideas are even linked in the remainder of 14:7: 'From now on, you do *know* him and have *seen* him.'

Moreover, John's Gospel is clearly concerned with how people move from seeing to knowing and believing (e.g. 20:24–31). Plenty of people lay eyes on Jesus without getting the point; they fail to 'see' him! One thoughtful commentator investigates John's verbs and concludes, 'In John, God is not so much invisible as unrecognized.'[13]

Similarly, John 1:18 is concerned as much with explaining God as seeing him. Encountering God is also in view in 1 John 4; 'seeing' God is nested within the wider concern of 'knowing' him (e.g. 4:7–8, 13, 16).

We must ask, then, why John's phrase is sometimes taken narrowly as a definitive statement about God's complete and permanent invisibility. Such interpreters seem to have been reading and emulating Plato and Justin Martyr. They need to reckon with Calvin,

---

13. Marianne Meye Thompson, '"God's Voice You Have Never Heard, God's Form You Have Never Seen": The Characterization of God in the Gospel of John', *Semeia* 63 (1993), p. 194.

who gets to the heart of the verse. 'When he says that none has seen God, it is not to be understood of the outward seeing of the physical eye.'[14] Major commentaries on John tend to concur, in part if not entirely.

We could explore John's details with ever finer precision, but it's beneficial to consider similar concerns in other passages. We should have seen enough to recognize (or recognized enough to see) that John does not set out to define God as strictly invisible and to tally the number who have not seen him. We misunderstand and misuse these texts if we hastily read them too literalistically and think they are sufficient to verify that 'Moses never saw God.'[15]

John 5:37

Defending against Jewish accusations, Jesus himself asserts concerning God the Father, 'You have never heard his voice nor seen his form.' Here is another verse that, at face value, seems to claim God's invisibility. As with the preceding Johannine texts, closer inspection suggests it does not actually render God unable to engage with his world. The verse does not require that we read Old Testament theophanies as christophanies.

Again the danger is taking the words too literalistically. Some who have done so have ended up insisting that, just as the Father has never been seen, so he has never been heard. That's what Jesus appears to say! But that interpretation claims too much. Regardless of what we make of God's appearing, there are plenty of occasions in both Old and New Testaments where his voice is experienced.

'The Old Testament is saturated with references to people who have heard God.'[16] Genesis, Exodus, Numbers and Judges are especially full of the everyday phrase 'God said'. The Ten Commandments are prefaced, 'And God spoke all these words, saying . . .' (Exod. 20:1 ESV). Another passage is similar: 'At once the LORD said

---

14. John Calvin, *The Gospel According to St John 1–10*, tr. T. H. L. Parker (Grand Rapids: Eerdmans, 1959), p. 25.

15. Kruse, *John*, p. 173.

16. Rodney A. Whitacre, *John*, IVPNTC 4 (Downers Grove: InterVarsity Press; Leicester: Inter-Varsity Press, 1999), p. 165.

to Moses, Aaron and Miriam . . . [H]e said, "Listen to my words . . ."'
(Num. 12:4, 6). We might also note that here God is said to descend
to meet them (in a pillar of cloud) and that he singles out Moses
because 'he sees the form of the LORD' (12:5, 8).

It's especially important to consider how God encounters Israel
at Mount Sinai. Hearing God is the whole point of the Sinai
theophany: 'The LORD said[!] to Moses, "I am going to come to you
in a dense cloud, so that the people will hear me speaking with you"'
(Exod. 19:9). The narrator confirms that this happens: 'Moses spoke
and the voice of God answered him' (19:19). When Moses recounts
the event later, it's precisely this audible encounter he highlights. In
three verses he affirms twice that God 'spoke' to the people, twice
that there was a 'sound/voice', and twice that the people 'heard' this
(Deut. 4:10, 12, 15). The people themselves confirm this, finding
God's voice terrifying (5:22–27). The audibility of God here in
Deuteronomy is even more significant because it also affirms that
the Israelites 'saw no form' of God on this occasion (4:12, 15); hence
this account is often understood to correspond closely with Jesus'
comments in John 5:37.

The last two paragraphs urge caution in explaining such passages.
In their enthusiasm to promote christophanies, interpreters can be
imprecise with their language and with the Bible's. A popular study
guide distributed through the influential London church associated
with John Stott exemplifies one such mistake. Evangelist Paul
Blackham correctly notes how Deuteronomy 4 attests that 'you
[Israelites] saw no form'. He then employs an *almost* identical phrase:
'no form was seen'. He reasons then that if 'no form was seen',
neither did Moses see anything. Blackham then extrapolates that
Moses *never* saw any form.[17] But God himself says in Numbers 12:8,
using the same noun, that Moses *did* see God's 'form' (and may even
suggest such a sighting was a regular, repeated experience). That the
Israelites were shielded from God's intensity on one occasion does
not entail that God permanently hides himself from everybody.

---

17. Paul Blackham, *A Study Guide to the Book of Exodus* (Carlisle: Authentic
    Lifestyle, 2003), pp. 31, 37; cf. Walter C. Kaiser Jr. (with others), *Hard
    Sayings of the Bible* (Downers Grove: InterVarsity Press, 1996), p. 155.

The New Testament confirms such audible encounters with God. These are more significant because they distinguish the speaking God from Jesus; it's the Father who is heard audibly by humans. At Jesus' baptism, at least Jesus and John hear the Father speak (Mark 1:11; John 1:33); Matthew's account hints that the voice addresses a wider listening audience (Matt. 3:17). The Father's voice at the transfiguration certainly addresses a plural audience; Matthew and Peter verify it was heard (Matt. 17:5–6; 2 Pet. 1:17–18). John's Gospel narrates another unique event where the Father speaks audibly, though it's less clear how much was comprehended (John 12:28–29).

Most christophany proponents are content to allow the Father to speak – just not to appear. Yet a surface reading of John 5:37 denies both. To his credit, one prominent proponent treats the verse consistently: 'God has never been either audible or visible.'[18] Hanson is right that the verse is equally strong about both seeing and hearing God. But this does not sit comfortably with either the christophany view or the uniform evidence for the Father's audibility. What then is Jesus claiming?

John 5:37 addresses a particular audience at one point in time. Jesus tells his contemporary opponents, 'You have failed to experience God as you should have.' Perhaps Jesus is contrasting these first-century Jews with their Israelite ancestors who certainly heard God's voice. More likely, as the surrounding verses suggest, Jesus is condemning his current opponents because they've failed to recognize and welcome the voice and form of God *as expressed in Jesus* (cf. 12:44–45; 14:9).

Just as Blackham is mistaken to generalize from the Sinai theophany, we would be mistaken to generalize from John 5:37. Blackham incorrectly moves from 'You [Israelites at Sinai] saw no form' to 'No human has ever seen God.' Neither should we move from 'You [stubborn first-century unbelievers] have never heard his voice nor seen his form' to 'God has never been either audible or visible.' We've already observed there were plenty of Israelites in both Old and New Testaments who heard God. Neither then can

---

18. Anthony Hanson, 'John i. 14–18 and Exodus xxxiv', *NTS* 23 (1976), p. 96.

this verse preclude the possibility that some of them saw God – as the Old Testament says some did.

Additionally, the wording of John 5:37 is very similar to that of John 1:18 and 1 John 4:12 (especially in Greek). The way we understand each verse should influence our understanding of the others. If 'You have never ... seen his form' does not demand God's permanent invisibility, we have further grounds to reconsider what John means by 'No one has ever seen God.'

John 6:46

One last verse in John is sometimes raised. What does Jesus mean when he insists, 'No one has seen the Father except the one who is from God; only he has seen the Father'?

The issue under discussion is how people come to Jesus and receive eternal life (e.g. 6:35–40). Thus in 6:46, like similar sentiments in 14:6–7, Jesus is challenging his opponents that there's no other way to find, to meet, to know, to 'see' God the Father. It's a statement about salvation, as reinforced even in the nearest verses (6:45, 47); it's not definitive of physically seeing God.

A literalistic sensory meaning, here as elsewhere, would render some statements nonsensical. Does Jesus naively use speech with deaf opponents ('you are unable to hear what I say', 8:43; cf. 8:47)? The earliest church fathers shrewdly asked how even the Son can see the Father if the Father is invisible. They too resolved that the simple sensory language here describes a more sophisticated encounter with God.

As a statement of salvation, the language of 'seeing' in 6:46 does not concern one's eyes. Like others in John, this verse should not be pressed to declare God completely and permanently invisible to visual perception. We've seen Thompson's summary that 'In John, God is not so much invisible as unrecognized.'[19] Elsewhere she elaborates on

> John's rendering of *seeing* both as a means of knowing God and as
> descriptive of the ultimate human encounter with God ... It is not that

---

19. Thompson, '"God's Voice"', p. 194.

God is 'invisible,' making sight physically impossible. Rather, God's holiness and majesty cannot be seen in their fullness by human beings. God may be seen in part, or indirectly.[20]

Colossians 1:15

It is Paul, perhaps citing an early Christian hymn, who introduces overt language of Jesus as 'the image of the invisible God'.

Although most Christians are familiar with the verse, we're often not exposed to important questions. Does 'God' here refer only to the Father? What does 'image' mean in biblical parlance? Is the Son '*the* image of God' or only '*an* image'? Is Paul describing eternity or only the incarnation (esp. 1:19)? How *then* should we perceive the word 'invisible'?

Generations of philosophy and theology safeguarding the Father, untainted from contact with his corrupt creation, hear here a claim of the Father's strict invisibility. Respected Bible translations and commentators infer a contrasting adjective: the Son is 'the *visible* image of the invisible God'.[21] We presume Paul is saying, 'The Son is the tangible representative of the ethereal Father.' We're not far from ancient world views or modern sci-fi where incorporeal deities or aliens have to recruit or infest a human as a mouthpiece.

The verse could actually mean 'The incarnate Jesus (a special work of the eternal Son) now speaks on behalf of the entire Trinity (whose prior interactions were relatively fleeting).' I'm not pushing every aspect of this interpretation, but it illustrates the flexibility of the terms involved.

Without exploring every nuance or offering further detail, I would suggest that this famous passage in Colossians does not contradict the visibility of God. Both the language of 'image' and

---

20. Marianne Meye Thompson, *The God of the Gospel of John* (Grand Rapids: Eerdmans, 2001), pp. 106, 113 (italics original).

21. NLT; GNB; Ben Witherington III, *The Letters to Philemon, the Colossians, and the Ephesians* (Grand Rapids: Eerdmans, 2007), p. 133; Murray J. Harris, *The Second Epistle to the Corinthians*, NIGTC (Grand Rapids: Eerdmans, 2005), p. 331.

'invisible/unseen' are sufficiently flexible to allow that God, even God the Father, has always been free to make his own visible forays into the world. Paul is here affirming something slightly different. He's rejoicing that the tangibility of the incarnate Son is orders of magnitude more intimate and permanent than any prior fleeting encounter with God. Through Jesus, people now engage with God more substantially in every sense (cf. Heb. 1:1–2).

Seen this way, there's nothing that requires the common super-ficial reading of Colossians 1:15. It does not somehow pit the visibility of the Son against the invisibility of the Father. We find here no concrete support that Old Testament theophanies must have been conducted, exclusively, by the Son. One commentary thus concludes carefully:

> If we consider the expression 'of God who is not seen' in light of the OT, then it becomes clear that we are not dealing primarily with the 'invisibility' of God and therefore not with the attempt to make him visible. Rather, the emphasis lies on the glory including the power of God which no human eye and no living person could withstand unless God himself provided special protection.[22]

Superlative language

We are starting to touch upon a phenomenon that comes to the fore in our remaining texts. Let's consider how superlative language works.

In generations gone by, students were taught rigid grammar. Where there are only two items in a set, you are supposed to use the 'comparative' not the 'superlative'. I am expected to refer to my two daughters as the 'elder' and 'younger', not the 'eldest' and 'youngest'. But most rules in most languages are progressively dis-regarded. Already this rule is waning and one day will be understood no better than the rule that makes a nonsense of supermarket checkout signs permitting 'ten items or less'. (I fear too few readers will comprehend what's wrong with such signs. Such unawareness is precisely my point!)

---

22. Barth and Blanke, *Colossians*, p. 250.

Greek once followed similar rules. But they too were starting to be ignored around the New Testament era. Jesus tells us the mustard seed 'is the smallest of all seeds' (Matt. 13:32), though Matthew formally writes only 'smaller'. Luke 9:48 could be translated woodenly as 'the *lesser* one among you is great', though most English Bibles correctly capture the intended sense of 'the *least* among all of you is the greatest' (NRSV). Comparing three major virtues, Paul concludes, 'the greatest of these is love' (1 Cor. 13:13) though, again, he actually writes only 'greater'. The exegetical implications of such examples are debated but the point remains that superlatives can be expressed through more than just the precise superlative terms.

The reverse also happens. A word that is technically superlative can be employed in ways that grammatical pedants could consider imprecise. Some scholars debate how Luke starts Acts. Technically, Luke may be describing his Gospel as 'the first book' (Acts 1:1 NRSV, ESV) of a series of *three* volumes (or more)! But most interpreters are content that, despite the apparent formality of the word, Luke simply means 'my former book' (NIV). Any imprecision is as inconclusive as when I slip into referring to my 'eldest' or 'youngest' daughter. Someone's language may not always encode the precision that others may expect.[23]

I raise these examples for the simple moral that we must be careful about inferring a degree of precision that is not implied.

There are many constructions in the Bible where grammatical pedantry may impose a degree of precision that is not intended. The book of Kings occasionally records excellent monarchs:

I will give you [Solomon] a wise and discerning heart, so that there will never have been anyone like you, nor will there ever be.
(1 Kgs 3:12; cf. 10:23)

Hezekiah trusted in the LORD, the God of Israel. There was no one like him among all the kings of Judah, either before him or after him.
(2 Kgs 18:5)

---

23. Cf. Craig S. Keener, *Acts* (Grand Rapids: Baker Academic, 2012), vol. 1, p. 651.

Neither before nor after Josiah was there a king like him who turned to
the LORD as he did.

(2 Kgs 23:25)

Who was the greatest king? The text of Scripture describes each of
these three as being unparalleled! The classic solution is to keep the
superlative language but constrain how it's applied. Solomon was
unequalled, with respect to wisdom. Hezekiah beat all contenders,
at trusting. We can count on one finger the king who best led the
nation in repentance, Josiah. We respect the numbering but nuance
its domain.

An alternative explanation is equally satisfying. Perhaps the author
is not trying to single out each king on a calculator or abacus. Perhaps
this is simply high praise for an elite group.[24]

We've all met excited teenagers who announce that today's
theme park or movie or celebrity encounter was the 'ultimate'
event. We recognize this as an expression of excitement – and not
one which evaluates that the rest of their lives will never again be
this good. Today's event was something really special but not
necessarily numerically unique. And our teens are almost certainly
not announcing their imminent deaths, even though 'ultimate'
formally means 'last'!

The author of Kings is probably doing the same. He is distinguishing these kings from the many lousy leaders who ruled God's
people. The exalted language ought not to be pressed so far as to
distinguish these kings from each other. Indeed it seems that, by
repeating such elite language, our author is actually *comparing* these
kings with each other. Describing them as 'unique' groups them
together, not tells them apart.

There are other examples of relative language in Scripture.
Authors pair 'love' and 'hate'. No one doubts there are times when
'to hate' really does mean 'to despise'. But there are several occasions

---

24. Much here is derived from Jerome H. Neyrey, '"First", "Only", "One
of a Few", and "No One Else": The Rhetoric of Uniqueness and the
Doxologies in 1 Timothy', *Bib* 86 (2005), pp. 59–87. Neyrey interacts
with other important scholarship.

where it simply means 'to love less' (e.g. Gen. 29:30–33; Deut. 21:15–17; Luke 14:26 ≈ Matt. 10:37).

I think it's this kind of language at work in the descriptions of the Father as 'invisible' and the Son as 'visible' in Colossians. It's not that one is never seen and the other one always. Rather, as in John, these are *relative* statements about the ease with which each is encountered. The same phenomenon also works well to describe the doxologies in 1 Timothy, to which we turn.

1 Timothy 1:17; 6:16

In the first and last chapters of this letter, Paul breaks into praise of 'the King eternal, immortal, invisible, the only God . . . who lives in unapproachable light, whom no one has seen or can see'. Once again, the New Testament seems to teach that God cannot be seen and, thus, has not been. Case closed?

I've just canvassed an alternative interpretation; this may be a way of praising God's excellence without fully defining him as *never* seen, never mortal, and so on. Thus we need to determine whether Paul is praising God this way because God *is* unique in all these respects or whether Paul is using this idiom as part of his rhetoric without intending the claims to be taken as absolutes.

Long story short: reading these as absolute claims creates many more difficulties than if we see them as a way of exalting God with superlative idioms. Consider the problems if we insist that Paul is being completely definitive.

The word 'only' recurs several times in these doxologies, praising 'the only God', 'the . . . only Ruler, the King of kings and Lord of lords, who alone [only] is immortal' (1:17; 6:15–16). We have to presume that Paul is describing God the Father; if the Son is addressed in any way, a new dilemma is created with the Son himself praised as 'invisible'! But then it's the Father who is the 'only Ruler'. Common sense tells us that the word 'only' is being used in a special way, not least because there are other human rulers named in Scripture (e.g. Luke 1:52; Acts 8:27). Moreover, the last book of the Bible says it's the resurrected Lamb – God the Son – who is the King of kings and Lord of lords (Rev. 1:5; 17:14; 19:16; cf. Jude 4).

And what does it mean that the Father is 'the only One who has immortality' (1 Tim. 6:16 HCSB)? Have we just denied the immortality of the Son and Spirit? Paul teaches elsewhere that our own mortal bodies look forward to 'immortality' and 'the imperishable' (1 Cor. 15:53–54), the same terms that belong 'only' to the Father according to 1 Timothy (though not always clear in English translations).

Rather, words like 'only' must have a relative sense. God is being contrasted with any potential rival and protected from any comparison. Paul 'affirms four truths about God's sovereign power, four ways in which he is altogether beyond human control or manipulation'.[25] In idol-filled Ephesus, where Timothy is ministering, pagans could approach and view their gods at any time. But the true God, by comparison, is unapproachable and invisible. Again we're dealing with relative language. As in the Old Testament and John's Gospel, Paul is emphasizing that our God cannot just be tracked down on a human whim. The Old and New Testaments affirm that God *can* be approached – though only rarely and under certain conditions, and now directly through Jesus. Relatively speaking, God is unapproachable. Relatively speaking, he is the only one who controls immortality. Relatively speaking, God is not seen. Although it can feel like a subtle distinction, 'contrasted with the visible' is not the same as saying 'never visible'.

And so the notion of the Father's invisibility – the foundational evidence for Old Testament theophanies being construed as christophanies – continues to evaporate. We've seen that some scholars sanction the possibility of such christophanies. So it's especially telling when those very same scholars will not press these doxologies to render the Father invisible – the very doxologies that not only describe him as 'invisible' but elaborate that he is the one 'whom no one has seen or can see'. Scholars admit that 'invisibility' language cannot be pressed to a literalistic, scientific kind of extreme. Jerome Neyrey's study of the rhetoric of these doxologies concludes that some superlative terms such as 'invisible' and 'unapproachable' emphasize 'God's *unknowability*, indicating that the most noble faculty of humans cannot approach, much less *comprehend* the deity'. He judges that these Greek terms are applied to God as testimony

---

25. John R. W. Stott, *The Message of 1 Timothy & Titus*, BST (Leicester: Inter-Varsity Press, 1996), p. 159.

'to the inability of the human mind to grasp or circumscribe him'. Neyrey demonstrates well that Paul is highlighting God's otherness and not formally defining attributes such as tangibility.[26] Anthony Hanson concedes even more when he concludes that, in these doxologies, 'There is no suggestion that God is naturally and essentially invisible.'[27]

It's puzzling that Neyrey and Hanson campaign for christophanies and God's invisibility based on John 1:18 when they don't press for God's invisibility here. After all, these Timothy doxologies move beyond saying 'No one has ever seen God' to actually describe him as 'invisible'. Further, the last phrase of 1 Timothy 6:16 closely resembles Exodus 33:20: both say that people 'are not able to see' God. We found that Exodus describes what Moses is (not) *permitted* to do, not what is (not) physically *possible*. So Borland and Kaiser are right to list Exodus 33:20 alongside verses such as John 1:18 and 1 Timothy 6:16, but they are wrong to conclude that such verses consistently teach God's permanent invisibility.

Hebrews 11:27

It would seem that the grounds on which we might consider God the Father to be invisible are progressively shrinking. So it would seem ill advised to build any kind of major edifice upon such a shaky and retreating foundation.

The short phrase in Hebrews need not detain us long. It's sometimes invoked because it applies *aoratos* to a divine figure in an Old Testament context.

One exhibit in the famous ancient hall of fame is Moses (Heb. 11:24–28). 'By faith he left Egypt, not fearing the king's anger; he persevered because he saw him who is invisible' (11:27). There are four problems with employing this phrase.

---

26. Neyrey, 'Rhetoric of Uniqueness', pp. 83, 84 (my italics). He touts christophanies, based on the Father's invisibility, in 'The Jacob Allusions in John 1:51', *CBQ* 44 (1982), pp. 590–591.

27. Anthony Tyrrell Hanson, *The Pastoral Epistles*, NCB (London: Marshall, Morgan & Scott, 1982), p. 113. Hanson advocates the Father's invisibility in 'John i. 14–18 and Exodus xxxiv', pp. 95–97.

First, Hebrews probably does not describe a real act of seeing. Despite the NIV's '*because* he saw', most interpreters and translations take the clause as hypothetical: '*as if* he saw'.

Secondly, what would it mean to 'see' someone 'invisible'? We cannot take both words in a literalistic fashion, and we've already seen(!) that such words have a range of metaphorical meanings. The rest of the chapter is about 'seeing' God's promises, even when prompts for faith are not always perceptible (e.g. 11:1, 6, 13). Scholars who brave the potential paradox in 11:27 conclude that it is a statement about Moses' 'spiritual perception'.[28] After all, he is being held up as one more example of what contemporary Christians *can* and should emulate, not what they cannot.

Thirdly, even though the verse is spotlighted by those seeking to promote the Father's invisibility, such a conclusion is coloured entirely by John and Paul. There's nothing in Hebrews that would identify the Invisible One as the Father. From Hebrews alone we would probably conclude that the author is speaking about Moses' seeing God in general or perhaps even seeing God the Son. After all, the preceding verse describes Moses' concern 'for the sake of Christ' (11:26) and this whole section culminates in a call to imitate the faith of such Old Testament heroes and to fix our eyes on Jesus (12:1–3). Those who are passionate about identifying Old Testament appearances of Jesus can thus get enthusiastic about 11:26 and 11:27. But they must then back-pedal lest they find themselves applying the term 'invisible' to the Son.

Finally, as we'll see in chapters 10 and 11, the language here tells us only how New Testament correspondents depict concepts such as 'the sake of Christ' and 'him who is invisible'. Such language furnishes no insight at all into what Moses himself perceived or understood.

Ultimately, few scholars put much weight at all on the occurrence of 'invisible' here. Most would concur that 'The translation "unseen" is preferable to "invisible".'[29]

---

28. Among others, see William L. Lane, *Hebrews 9–13*, WBC 47B (Waco: Word, 1991), p. 376.

29. David L. Allen, *Hebrews*, NAC 35 (Nashville: B & H, 2010), p. 561.

Summary of New Testament passages

The New Testament authors are excited to praise the incarnation of God the Son as Jesus the Messiah. They rightly celebrate that access to God is now so much greater than the old covenant formerly afforded. In such an exuberant context we can appreciate why some of their language might sound as if it makes absolute claims about the Father's inaccessibility.

If, however, such language proves to be a rhetorical generalization or relativization, we ought not to press it to mean that the Father has always been and remains entirely inaccessible and invisible.

As we move towards this synthesis, it's important to remember that the New Testament itself accepts the possibility of seeing God. Some passages look forward to a time when God the Father *can* be seen (Matt. 5:8; 1 Cor. 13:12; Heb. 12:14; 1 John 3:2; Rev. 22:4). Even allowing that such language itself is probably figurative to some degree, there is no reason to conclude that the Father is permanently imperceptible to human eyes. Certainly, such verses talk of 'seeing God' and must be kept in view when we wrestle with those that speak against 'seeing God'.

We've also seen texts that talk of the Son's seeing the Father (esp. John 6:46). Elsewhere, Jesus himself affirms that the 'angels' of childlike disciples 'continually see the face of my Father in heaven' (Matt. 18:10 NRSV). We might also wonder what Paul himself saw and heard in the 'visions and revelations' he mentions in passing (2 Cor. 12:1–4). Once again the impression is given that there's something of the Father to be seen. It's just not on regular display, especially when contrasted with the ready visibility of the incarnate Son.

For now – and despite the impression often conveyed – we can simply observe that the New Testament does not cast a monolithic shadow across the possibility of seeing God. We ought not to conclude from the New Testament that he can never be seen, and we should certainly not pit the New Testament against the Old Testament as if it somehow definitively trumps the language there of seeing God. Although further alleged passages are considered in part 3, it does not yet appear that the New Testament requires us to interpret Old Testament theophanies as christophanies.

4. TOWARD A DOCTRINE OF (IN)VISIBILITY

As a new generation rebels against scientific modernity and rediscovers the spiritual and supernatural, the unseen realm is once again of interest alongside seen reality. Certainly the rise of science-fictional and fantasy genres contributes as we speculate playfully about the adventures of characters who can prowl unseen by others. They're freed from the binding rules of nature. Many heroes and superheroes can control their visibility with a magic cloak, a rationed potion, a precious ring, an esoteric incantation or a genetic mutation. Invisibility is a temporary and volitional choice.

God is not always extended the same courtesy. When they consider the question, many theologians do allow that God can temporarily and volitionally render himself visible. That's the conclusion towards which we're moving. But many capable, articulate, prominent scholars don't reach this conclusion; we've seen some representative examples. Too many don't even consider the question.

Considering the question allows us to glean something positive from our investigation. At the same time as casting doubt on the likelihood of Old Testament christophanies, we find that we're enhancing our thinking about God and how he engages the world he created. We can affirm that God remains interested in his world and interactive with it, and perhaps even that God the Father might be said to be encountered visibly.

What the Bible is not saying

I hesitate to find Old Testament appearances of the preincarnate Son, certainly not in the sense that he is acting distinctly from the other members of the Trinity. I think any evidence in favour of Old Testament christophanies has been greatly overestimated. But I must not be misunderstood as uninterested in the importance or magnificence of the person of the Trinity who became incarnate in Jesus. Along with the Father and Spirit, the Son remains at the centre of the Christian gospel. Each of the New Testament passages we've skimmed shares this adoration and exaltation. The Son's incarnation has rendered the triune God far more tangible and intimate than at any prior time. So it's thoroughly appropriate that they and we celebrate Jesus as the most complete encounter with God.

This celebration discovers that comparative language is sometimes inadequate. Humanity's encounter with God, in and through and by and as Jesus, is on many fronts so superior that comparative language rightly gives way to superlative. But we must be careful to recognize when superlative language is a qualitative expression of exuberance rather than a quantitative measure of science.

Again, native speakers of English know how to discern when literal terms have been appropriated in non-literal ways. We've all met (or been) an exasperated parent or friend or employer; we know firsthand the cry 'I've told you a million times . . .'; we all accept this as a valid communication – even though 'a million' is not intended in its strict numerical sense. Such emotive hijacking of literal terms fills the daily conversations of young and old: 'you're the *greatest*'; 'I'm *never* speaking to you again'; 'that was the *best* meal *ever*'. The superlative claims made in advertising echo and cement such language.

So we need to be alert to occasions where the biblical languages are doing the same. We've found reasons to interpret the superlative language of Scripture as sometimes figurative rather than mathematically definitive, as qualitative rather than quantitative. The New

Testament authors exhibit this trend when they promote the incarnation in grand terms.

Certainly, we've found grounds on which the word 'invisible' may be better understood as 'unseen'. The Greek term *aoratos* explains that something is not in view, but it does not clarify why viewing is not feasible. Thus one seasoned commentator on Colossians 1:15 is quite right to observe that the adjective 'is used to describe not merely what has not been seen (= unseen) but also what cannot be seen by mortal sight (= invisible; as also in v. 16)'.[1] But he is too hasty to presume which sense is in view here.

Thus it's incumbent upon Bible readers of all standards to consider how to approach New Testament texts that appear to present God the Father as invisible. We're motivated all the more by the consistent testimony of the Old Testament that God can be seen (whether or not he always avails himself of the opportunity).

What the Bible does suggest

We've observed some reputable scholars who, through haste or convenience or convention, accept the familiar and literal sense that 'God is invisible.' It's pleasing to discover that, when time or space allows, scholars can present a more nuanced summary of the issue. What they discover is that God is invisible *to human probing.* God's 'invisibility' is not a scientific constant that applies symmetrically to divine and human parties. Such asymmetry may surprise those of us who assume or aspire to a world that is more egalitarian and/or scientifically consistent.

Various theologians express God's complete control over nature and how he engages with and through it. This is especially true of those whose task is to collate and systematize all of Scripture on a given topic; we'll meet several 'systematic theologians' in the coming paragraphs. That God retains complete control over his visual interactions is expressed clearly by Reformed thinker Herman Bavinck:

---

1. Murray J. Harris, *Colossians & Philemon*, EGGNT (Nashville: B & H Academic, 2010), p. 39.

'God is invisible but is able to make himself visible and to reveal himself to man. "It is not in our power to see him but it is in his power to reveal himself."[2]

Concerned with christophanies or not, theologians start investigating God's (in)visibility with John 4:24. There Jesus talks about the Father and affirms that 'God is spirit.' The same world view that made Justin Martyr consider the Father as utterly transcendent can bring us to assume that here is a definition of God's body – or, more precisely, his lack of one. But that is too simplistic a reading of the verse, as any commentary will demonstrate. John 4:24 does not define God's tangibility any more than does 1 John 1:5 ('God is light') or Hebrews 12:29 ('God is a consuming fire', an image drawn from the Old Testament). 'To say that God is invisible and spiritual does not suggest that he is limited to the invisible and spiritual, excluded from the visible, material and physical.'[3]

The more transcendent view of deity, as articulated by Justin and echoed by church thinkers for several centuries, was more indebted to Greek philosophy than to Scripture. The idea remains entrenched in many parts of the church today, now affected (if not infected) by both Greek and Christian traditions. Such entrenched traditions leave God the Father somehow *confined* to his transcendence. The better solution is to allow that God *controls* any interactions with his world. God may be seen if he wants to be seen.

Indeed, the tradition of God's invisibility has not been universal. Bavinck's summary above concludes with a quote from the fourth-century bishop Ambrose: 'It is not in our power to see him but it is in his power to reveal himself.' The asymmetry is important, especially in granting God full sovereignty over theophanies.

---

2. Herman Bavinck, *The Doctrine of God* (Grand Rapids: Eerdmans, 1951), pp. 180–183 (quote on p. 181).

3. Donald G. Bloesch, *God the Almighty* (Downers Grove: InterVarsity Press, 1995), p. 90. Wesley Williams's excursus traces how thinkers such as Plato conflated 'invisible' with 'incorporeal' and affirms that this is not a biblical equation ('*Tajallī wa-Ru'ya*: A Study of Anthropomorphic Theophany and *Visio Dei* in the Hebrew Bible, the Qur'ān and Early Sunnī Islam' [PhD diss., University of Michigan, 2008], pp. 30–34).

Virtually the same words are found in the same period from the famous theologian Augustine. And the same sentiment can be found two centuries earlier. Not long after Justin, the second-century bishop Irenaeus wrote, 'For man does not see God by his own powers; but when He pleases He is seen by men, by whom He wills, and when He wills, and as He wills.'[4]

God's sovereign control over theophanies is entirely consistent with Scripture. It can be demonstrated from clearer passages and helps to explain others.

Any theophany requires a degree of 'accommodation': God tones down his full essence for human consumption. We see this accommodation illustrated in (but not limited to) many examples where God wraps himself in a cloud or in darkness or in some human guise. He hides Moses from the full force of his 'face' (Exod. 33:18–23). This is important because some christophany proponents, such as Justin, claim an in-principle objection against such accommodation. Yet accommodation is a central tenet of the Son's incarnation. Jesus is an adequate encounter with God (e.g. John 12:45; 14:9) but does not provide an exhaustive experience of God. We know that Jesus was at times transfigured beyond his usual human appearance (Mark 9:2–3) even to the point of not being visibly recognizable (Luke 24:16; John 20:14; 21:4). Jesus himself confirmed that his disciples had not yet 'seen' his full glory (John 17:24). We can certainly understand the Bible's expectation that there's more to experience of God one day.

God's control is exhibited on occasions when he chooses *not* to accommodate himself. Much of the Old Testament is about the different levels of access that God is willing to grant, including warnings against encountering him *without his approval*. The Israelites at Sinai are not to breach the security perimeter at this summit meeting, while Moses and some of the leaders are granted entry (Exod. 19:20–22; 24:9–11). No one should brave God's manifestation above the ark in the Most Holy Place, though the high priest

---

4. Respectively, Ambrose, *Exposition of Luke* 1.26 (CSEL 32.4.27); Augustine, Letter 147.18 (PL 33.3); Irenaeus, *Against Heresies* 4.20.5 (*ANF* 1:489).

is invited in once each year after stringent preparation (Lev. 16:1–2). The Levites who carry this portable tabernacle must not glimpse or touch the sacred furniture, though their priestly cousins may (Num. 4:15–20). Although it's right to be distressed, we ought not to be surprised when God's fiery wrath flares out against those who flout his terms and conditions (Lev. 10:1–4; 1 Sam. 6:19; 2 Sam. 6:1–8; 1 Chr. 13:9–11; 15:11–15). Our dismay indicates how comfortable we've become with the many occasions when God graciously chooses to accommodate himself and waive the expectation of death.

The book of Esther offers a helpful parallel. The Persian ruler enjoys unparalleled power and prestige (Esth. 1:1–8). Seven nobles 'had special access to the king' (1:14). This 'special access' is a modern way of expressing the idiom with which we've been concerned: these are the seven elite princes 'who saw the king's face' (1:14 ESV). A similar description is found just a few verses earlier, naming the seven eunuchs who 'served the face of the king' (1:10, my tr.; cf. 1 Sam. 2:18). Later in Esther's story we hear again that access to the king is extremely privileged. You're either summoned or you hope desperately that he's in a good mood and grants an audience by extending his sceptre (4:11). Esther repeatedly gains such favour (5:2; 8:3–4). It's barging into the king's presence *without his approval* that's fatal.

So, too, with the illustration that opened chapter 2. Especially in the interpretative novelization of the scene, Admiral Piett ponders if anyone else has ever sighted Darth Vader unmasked. Quite reasonably he worries that his unwonted experience may prove short-lived.

The story of Scripture is that God is regularly merciful on such occasions (though not all). He is willing and even enthusiastic to accept the unworthy into his presence and accommodates himself accordingly. Sometimes he invites them nearer to his throne room. Other theophanies depict God's venturing out among his people, guarding fallen humanity from his effects on them and not holding them liable for his initiative. As Christians attest, the incarnation is the most profound and enduring example.

This solution, that leaves God the final arbiter of both the cause and effect of theophanies, is articulated well by some systematic theologians. We've seen Bavinck's helpful summary. Another massive study of God revisits and elaborates Bavinck's position. The highlights of John Frame's conclusion encapsulate well both Bavinck's point and several of the other issues we've been considering:

> 1. God is *essentially invisible.* This means, not that he can never be seen under any circumstances, but rather that, as Lord, he sovereignly chooses when, where, and to whom to make himself visible . . .
>
> 2. God has often made himself visible, in theophany and in the incarnate Christ, so that human beings may on occasion truly say that they have 'seen God.' . . .
>
> 3. 'No one has ever seen God' (John 1:18a) means that no one has ever seen God apart from his voluntary theophanic-incarnational revelation . . .
>
> 4. It is right to be terrified in the presence of theophany . . . But, as we have seen, some people do see God without losing their lives.[5]

Although often with less detail, a similar conclusion can be found from other theologians at different points of the scholarly and denominational spectrums.[6]

These theologians tend to be generalists, summarizing many facets of God. It's equally important to recognize that the same conclusion is endorsed by scholars who delve specially into theophanies. Three studies suffice for now, again representing various confessional

---

5. John M. Frame, *The Doctrine of God* (Phillipsburg: P & R, 2002), p. 590; cf. his *Systematic Theology: An Introduction to Christian Belief* (Phillipsburg: P & R, 2013), p. 672. Note the Reformed and Presbyterian confessional positions of Bavinck and Frame. A strong commitment to a unified salvation between Old and New Testaments can lead thinkers from these traditions to emphasize christophanies.

6. I collate a sample in the final footnotes of my 'The Invisibility of God: A Survey of a Misunderstood Phenomenon', *EvQ* 79 (2007), pp. 328–329. After Frame, perhaps the next most important and detailed study is John S. Feinberg, *No One Like Him: The Doctrine of God* (Wheaton: Crossway, 2001), pp. 214–224.

concerns. They also helpfully pinpoint the relevance of Exodus 33:20, its apparent threat of death, and the solution of God's volition.

One scholar who specializes in the appearances of Middle Eastern gods captures things succinctly:

> God may reveal himself whenever and to whomever he wishes . . .
> [I]t is common to find people dying not because they have seen God
> but because they have not followed the rules in approaching him.[7]

Another famous Old Testament scholar and linguist resolves that

> it is only exceptionally therefore, and to special persons, that God makes
> himself visible; when he does, as Manoah's wife reasons, one may
> suppose that he would not have gone to so much bother if it were only
> to put them to death.[8]

And a more detailed study of the biblical phrase 'face to face' yields a very careful summary indeed:

> When Yahweh proclaims 'humanity cannot see [i.e., look at] me and
> live', he is prohibiting Moses from being the active agent in seeing the
> divine face, but this statement does not prohibit Yahweh from revealing
> his face to a human. In other words, Yahweh may actively reveal himself
> to whomever he chooses (as he does in each of the 'face to face'
> encounters), but the human is the passive recipient of this revelation,
> not the active agent.[9]

---

7. Samuel A. Meier, 'Theophany', in Bruce M. Metzger and Michael D. Coogan (eds.), *The Oxford Companion to the Bible* (New York: Oxford University Press, 1993), p. 740.

8. James Barr, 'Theophany and Anthropomorphism in the Old Testament', in *Congress Volume: Oxford 1959*, VTSup 7 (Leiden: Brill, 1960), p. 34.

9. Ian Douglas Wilson, '"Face to Face" with God: Another Look', *ResQ* 51 (2009), p. 112, n. 23 (his square brackets). I have simplified Wilson's Hebrew phrases.

The crucial question for christophanies

It seems to me that those campaigning for christophanies have trouble integrating all the biblical evidence and various interpretative possibilities. Christophanies are presented and defended by ignoring or sacrificing one or more of these.

James Borland cites the 'volitional' solution promoted by Barr and several others. This accords well with Borland's own definition that theophanies are unsought by their human recipients. Yet he is frustratingly inconsistent with his treatment of the 'invisibility' texts. A later chapter allows that they proscribe only a full sighting of God and that some kind of visible manifestation can be permitted. But the preceding chapter relies upon such texts to distinguish tentatively between appearances of Father and Son, supposedly proving the former unlikely and the latter preferable.[10] As we'll see in coming chapters, the evidence adduced for favouring the Son against the Father by Borland – who remains arguably the key proponent of christophanies and the catalyst for their recent popularity – is terribly slender. For those hoping to emulate his enthusiasm, it's disturbing and deflating that he substantially undermines his own position in at least three ways: (1) he accepts invisibility to be an attribute of God the Son also, but one that the Son can relinquish for the sake of theophanies; (2) he concedes that 'the Father and the Holy Spirit are *nearly* always characterized by the attribute of immateriality' but can relinquish this sufficiently to generate physical manifestations; (3) he ultimately resolves:

> It is not possible for God to be *confined* to a particular form . . . These [invisibility texts] must express the impossibility of seeing God *in His existence form*, for the balance of Scripture also indicates that God may *purpose* to exhibit Himself in some physical way. To see such a *manifestation* of Him is not fatal nor scripturally incongruent with God's invisibility.[11]

---

10. James A. Borland, *Christ in the Old Testament*, 2nd ed. (Fearn: Mentor, 1999), e.g. pp. 85–86, 98–99 versus pp. 57–58, 62.

11. Ibid., respectively pp. 20, 62 (my italics), 85–86 (italics original).

Inconsistency or incompleteness marks and mars others' arguments as well, further suggesting that the interpretation of Old Testament theophanies as christophanies cannot be sustained. We've already noted Paul Blackham's mistake in rephrasing 'you saw no form' as 'no form was seen', especially when passages such as Numbers 12:8 affirm that God's 'form' was sometimes seen. Other interpreters want to pin down individual words and fail to recognize that these are not always treated uniformly. Yes, Moses demands to see God's glory and is unable to withstand it (Exod. 33:18–23; 40:34–35). Yet at other times the same 'glory' can be witnessed by Moses (Num. 20:6) and even by all Israel (Exod. 16:10; Lev. 9:23; Num. 14:10; Deut. 5:24). When Korah and other leaders rebel, we find twice that God's 'glory' appears to all Israel and is *selective* in consuming only some of them in judgment (Num. 16:19, 42).

For those who would champion christophanies, the heart of the matter can be distilled to a single question with many doctrinal consequences. What is the difference between God the Father and the preincarnate Son that supposedly renders one of them impervious to human sight while the other makes regular appearances? An answer is not nearly as forthcoming as some would suggest.

Room for improvement

Although it's tempting to insist that christophanies are completely ruled out and that God the Father is certainly involved in every Old Testament theophany, that would be to claim more than the evidence (so far) can bear. It's possible that the members of the Trinity might *choose* for the Son to be their visual representative. This, however, is a line of argument not often pursued to support christophanies. Where it's hinted at, it tends to be argued with the same kind of superficial treatment as the other passages surveyed. It may be suggested (along lines similar to Calvin) that there is only 'one mediator between God and mankind, the man Christ Jesus' (1 Tim. 2:5). That misunderstands the word 'mediator'. It's invoked because it sounds like the Son is the one person who *speaks* for God. However, its meaning in the Bible (and even typically in the Reformers) primarily concerns the *reconciliation* effected by Jesus.

This understanding is available even in the most accessible Bible dictionaries. The Son's reconciling mediation, of course, offers no clarity on who makes visible appearances in theophanies.[12]

We've certainly found that the usual grounds for ruling out the Father's involvement are shaky. This should give us confidence in reclaiming the importance of the Father, arguably the member of the Trinity persistently overlooked in many Christian traditions. Studies of the Father from an evangelical perspective seem especially lacking.[13]

It's ironic that christophany proponents universally seek to defend conservative doctrines of the Trinity against more liberal distortions. They seek to honour the person and work of our triune God. Yet we might better honour the Trinity, and God the Father in particular, if we recognize the possibility of his direct engagement with the created world.

Proponents are also keen to teach readers to interpret the Bible, to solicit its underlying reality (especially concerning the Trinity's interactions with the world), and to praise and worship God better. I heartily commend these goals! Yet our investigation of God's invisibility suggests that several interpretive steps are superficial. An inadequate treatment of New Testament passages can become an entirely misleading guide to Old Testament texts.

The exegetical shortcomings for both testaments are fuelled by a particular doctrinal framework that needs revisiting. We've seen that Justin Martyr was concerned to defend God in a post-biblical era that prided itself on God's transcendence. Similar strands of Greek philosophy continue to influence biblical interpreters today;

---

12. For sources concerning 'mediator', see my analysis of 'Paul Blackham
    1: Weak Exegetical Links', *Chm* 125 (2011), pp. 62–63 and endnotes.

13. One rare volume might be Thomas A. Smail, *The Forgotten Father*, 2nd
    ed. (London: Hodder & Stoughton, 1987). The promising title by
    Christopher J. H. Wright, *Knowing God the Father Through the Old
    Testament* (Oxford: Monarch, 2007), is disappointing when it focuses
    on parental aspects of God and not on the first person of the Trinity.
    The popular BST series offers volumes on *The Message of the Person of
    Christ* and *of the Holy Spirit*, but not (yet) *The Message of God the Father*.

one barely differs from Justin in insisting that 'Scripture is very
definite in its statements that there has never been an immediate
revelation of the supermundane Deity (see John 1:18 and I Tim.
6:16), and He has never made a temporary descent into visibility.'[14]
Well might we complain that 'the conservatives themselves have
sometimes been too unaware of how far they have "sold out" to
Greek philosophical traditions'.[15] As with any topic of interpretation, the question of God's (in)visibility can teach us to read the
Scriptures better. The relevant New Testament texts were themselves
addressed to specific cultures and they used their words in specific
ways to achieve specific ends. We're called to investigate those ways
and ends before we superficially apply and obey them today.

More extensive analysis may well present a whole-Bible approach
to God's involvement with the world that is the *opposite* of what the
Bible has sometimes been thought to teach. Scripture was once
considered to endorse prevailing practices of slavery, but most
Christians now concur that slave-oriented passages should not be
interpreted and applied to that end. Likewise, if we can sufficiently
resist any cultural influences pushing for a completely transcendent
God, the Judeo-Christian world view may even more clearly teach
something quite distinguishable: the story of a God who, although
transcendent, dares to get his hands dirty interacting with his
creation.

None of this should be misunderstood as detracting from the
incarnation. Indeed, I would think it enhances that pinnacle of God's
redemptive work if we determine that God has always been able
and willing to encounter humanity through a variety of personal and
volitional interactions. The incarnation constitutes the zenith of
God's repeated and direct and tangible interactions with the world.

There are, of course, many further implications that flow from
such a conclusion. An enhanced view of God's interactivity with
the world invites us also to consider the created order as of more

---

14. Daniel G. Finestone, 'Is the Angel of Jehovah in the Old Testament
    the Lord Jesus Christ?', *BSac* 95 (1938), p. 376.
15. D. A. Carson, *How Long, O Lord?*, 2nd ed. (Grand Rapids: Baker
    Academic, 2006), p. 166, concerned with a different misapplication.

significance than it enjoys under many world views. The same Greek philosophy that attempted to shield God the Father from getting his hands and feet dirty tended (and sometimes still tends) to denigrate the merit of nature. In turn, an enhanced view of the value of creation will impact how we view the pending 'new heavens and new earth', contributing to the question of whether these will replace or renovate the cosmos we currently inhabit. In turn, this will influence our response to contemporary ecological crises and to doctrinal and pastoral approaches to the intermediate state of those who have died. All sorts of other questions might be approached with fresh eyes as we ask what God is like and what it means for humanity to be created in and conformed to his 'image'.

Summary of part 1

We've not actually dispensed with Old Testament christophanies. As we consider this interesting but contentious interpretation, there may be no 'knockdown argument' one way or the other.

Certainly, I have no intention of committing the same injustice against the Son that I feel is sometimes perpetrated against the Father. It remains entirely plausible, theologically, that God the Son was involved in Old Testament theophanies. As proponents helpfully remind us, it would indeed be consistent with his pending involvement in the incarnation.

But can we insist that he is the sole participant in such theophanies? The foundational argument at most points of church history has been that this is likely because of the Father's invisibility. I am calling this alleged invisibility into question. As long as the allegation of invisibility remains weak or unproven, we cannot extol the likelihood of exclusive christophanies.

Christians agree that God has communicated with his world in many and varied ways. Among these there's no shortage of visual phenomena. Theophanies are a significant part of the Bible's message, and no one doubts the sheer breadth of their attestation or the uniform way in which they are presented as tangible, sensory encounters with God. Wesley Williams summarizes many studies when he concludes:

> The motif of 'seeing God' or of God's 'appearing' to man is distributed across the literary units and genres of the Bible . . . The God of Israel was theophanous: he was wont to visibly appear to certain individuals and, more rarely, groups under special conditions.[16]

Any evidence for *not* seeing God is slim indeed. It's concentrated in a small number of New Testament texts where the idea of 'invisibility' is best understood as a culturally appropriate way of depicting God as 'beyond common earthly experience'. Christian tradition, transparently abetted at various stages by the popularity of Greek philosophy, has regularly allowed these few texts to dominate and direct biblical interpretation. Even a limited analysis of these passages suggests that it may be these few New Testament words and phrases, rather than any other biblical doctrines or interpretations, that need to be reconsidered.

In investigating God's appearances, we have had to consider a little more about the nature of theophanies in general. In particular, we must affirm that every theophany is an accommodation on God's part; there's no suggestion that any sighting of God – whether of Father or Son or Spirit – is an exhaustive experience of the Trinity. 'While the essential characteristic of every theophany is the appearance of God, in every theophany God's power must be held in check.'[17] This applies as much to the Son's incarnation as to any other manifestation of any member of the Trinity.

In the light of all this, we find that one of the primary arguments for interpreting Old Testament theophanies as exclusive christophanies is substantially challenged. Assumptions about the utter invisibility of the Father do not appear to stand up under scrutiny. To the contrary, we may do better to recognize that what are sometimes narrowly defined as christophanies were actually theophanies in a fuller sense.

---

16. Williams, 'Anthropomorphic Theophany and *Visio Dei*', pp. 27, 29, singling out the Hebrew verb *r'h*.

17. Mark F. Rooker, 'Theophany', in *DOTP*, p. 861.

PART 2

IS JESUS THE ANGEL OF THE LORD?

5. LIKELY SUSPECTS

Despite being only a modest size, my local church is overrun with twins. The prospect of children's ministry is daunting when there are at least seven pairs of twins waiting to be distinguished!

Our society has always relished the mischief that can be wrought when individuals are hard to tell apart. I grew up with the story of *The Five Chinese Brothers*, interchangeable siblings who each uses his superpower to escape some drastic execution. Disney engages young audiences with mix-and-match escapades such as *The Parent Trap*. And there have been endless other variations of Mark Twain's *The Prince and the Pauper*.

Distinguishing near-identical figures is the key issue when we consider the enigmatic figure called 'the Angel of the Lord'. Having determined (for whatever reason) that the triune Son makes visible appearances in the Old Testament, the Angel is the individual almost always singled out as Exhibit A. He is supposed to be incontrovertible evidence of a Godlike figure who walks among humans.

The arguments of the previous part and this one are closely linked, though they are not logically dependent upon each other.

Detective stories seek to establish which possible perpetrator had both motive and opportunity to commit a felony. When it comes to Old Testament christophanies, the invisibility of God the Father is a central motive for considering the Son's involvement; encounters with the Angel of the Lord are seen as those opportunities being taken.

Making the case

In detective stories, the sleuth has to work hard at establishing that a potential opportunity was indeed exploited. Too many modern attempts at the genre become tedious precisely because nearly every suspect has viable motive and opportunity! So it's incumbent to move beyond circumstantial evidence in order to substantiate whether the suspicious-looking butler is in fact guilty or merely a red herring.

The same rigour is required of those who promote christophanies. They are almost universal in their dependence upon the Angel of the Lord for illustrating their case. But a plausible illustration or hypothesis is insufficient evidence in itself. Good detectives have to marshal adequate positive evidence to substantiate their suspicion. They also have to accommodate any inconvenient negative evidence that threatens to exonerate the suspect. By exploring such evidence in greater depth, part 2 proposes that christophany proponents are found wanting on both counts. We cannot safely single out the Angel from a line-up; there is not the proverbial 'smoking gun' that confirms guilt; the most likely suspects are red herrings; we don't have sufficient evidence for conviction.

Because most of the evidence is circumstantial, christophany proponents are a little more diverse in how they introduce and identify the Angel. Nonetheless, their diverse presentations usually approximate a three-stage syllogism similar to the one shown in part 1. The argument runs like this:

1. The Angel of the Lord is hard to distinguish from God himself, but
2. the Angel does sometimes seem to be distinct, therefore

3. we need to explain an individual who is simultaneously God and not God.[1]

Such an issue is obviously of great value to those seeking to find the Son in the Old Testament. Several encounters with the Angel are narrated. And who best fits the identikit profile of 'simultaneously God and not God'? We can see why the conclusion at point 3 is so enthusiastically presented to any wavering jury. Once again, this enthusiastic solution can be traced back at least as far as Justin Martyr in the second century.

The issue also besets any biblical commentator who has to explain the Angel. Especially prominent Angel accounts occur in Genesis 16, Exodus 3, Numbers 22, Judges 2, 6 and 13, and Zechariah 3; we'll investigate these and others in due course. Commentators on such passages are not usually commissioned to prove point 3, but they do scrutinize the evidence for points 1 and 2.

Like good trial juries, and ideally just as impartially, we need to look at the evidence being presented before we can validate the conviction being pushed for. What evidence is there in the Old Testament for a figure who is 'simultaneously God and not God'?

Likely suspects

Some fictional detectives have the luxury of being able to investigate the evidence entirely objectively. Sherlock Holmes or Hercule Poirot returns home to his isolated apartment, mulls over the interesting fragments he has gleaned, and then proceeds to pronounce that the perpetrator is of a certain height and build, and enjoys a particular vocation and personal habits. Having determined the theoretical description, our detective sets out to identify which individual fits it.

But many crime bureaus and courtrooms take a more pragmatic approach. There are only a finite number of suspects, and the forces

---

1. E.g. Ron Rhodes, *Christ Before the Manger: The Life and Times of the Preincarnate Christ* (Grand Rapids: Baker, 1992), p. 80.

of law and order have limited time and resources to rule out some and narrow down the list to one.

We face the same dilemma. An ideal study of the Angel of the Lord would start from first principles. It would build up a theoretical description and then (and only then) attempt to see if anyone fits it. But this debate has raged for two centuries and there are few impartial juries available who have not already heard something of the plausible suspects. Neither do I have unlimited space to present the ideal exhaustive study.

Instead, let us advance the process and parade the shortlist of most likely suspects. These have been proposed throughout church history and each has been more popular among certain groups and at certain times. An introduction to each candidate will help us to assess the evidence efficiently, which we'll inspect in successive chapters.

I'm choosing to simplify this line-up of suspects to just three. As we'll see, they coincide roughly with the three syllogism emphases listed above as 1, 2 and 3. Their popularity, however, comes largely in reverse order. We'll build up to Candidate 3, whose identification is arguably the most favoured in conservative circles and appears to clinch christophanies.

While inducting the jury, I should flag three further matters. First, the suspects go under a number of aliases. The Old Testament version of the phrase is usually printed as 'the Angel of the LORD' in Bibles. The capitalized 'LORD' refers to God's personal name, 'Yahweh' or 'Jehovah'. So the titles 'the Angel of the Lord' and 'the Angel of Yahweh' are interchangeable. Some Bible texts use a different word, naming 'the Angel of God'; that is also interchangeable. I choose to capitalize 'Angel' to distinguish our special case from several other angels in the Bible, though you won't find such capitals in the original languages or in most English translations. Secondly, any official descriptions used for labelling the three candidates vary from scholar to scholar. I've tried to avoid getting tangled in any set of particular terms. Thirdly, I refer to the Angel as 'he'. This is purely from convention and does not assume a sex for this Angel. Nor can it sway the jury towards one candidate or another, for all three are readily and regularly described in masculine terms.

Candidate 1

The primary trait that singles out the Angel of the Lord from other Old Testament characters is that on many occasions he is hard to distinguish from the Lord himself. Scholars regularly show the similarities, with the Angel's speaking and behaving as if he were Yahweh. This point is not disputed. The Angel has attracted so much attention precisely because everyone recognizes this considerable overlap.

Those who favour christophanies certainly concur. It's a substantial part of the case they build. For example, James Borland develops the rest of his book from a chapter concerning the Angel. That chapter begins with absolute certainty that the Angel is God:

> In many instances where Christophanies occurred in the Old Testament, the person who appeared is called 'the angel of the LORD.' . . . It is the thesis of this chapter that 'the angel of the LORD' is the same person as 'the LORD.' Both are to be understood as appearances of God Himself in human form.[2]

Whatever else might be said about the Angel, the overlap with God is readily recognized and accepted.

It's not hard to find compilations of the evidence favouring this identification. Commentaries on Angel passages regularly rehearse the data.[3] Cross-references in the influential *Dictionary of the Old Testament* advise enquirers that the 'Angel of the Lord' is best consulted under matters of 'Theophany' and 'Divine Presence'.[4] Thus the first possible solution is that 'the Angel of the Lord' is just another of several titles employed to describe God.

---

2. James A. Borland, *Christ in the Old Testament: Old Testament Appearances of Christ in Human Form*, 2nd ed. (Fearn: Mentor, 1999), p. 35.

3. See e.g. the helpful table of data and history of interpretation compiled by John H. Walton, *Genesis*, NIVAC (Grand Rapids: Zondervan, 2001), pp. 462–464.

4. *DOTP*, p. 37; Tremper Longman III and Peter Enns (eds.), *Dictionary of the Old Testament: Wisdom, Poetry & Writings* (Downers Grove: InterVarsity Press; Nottingham: Inter-Varsity Press, 2008), p. 13.

Candidate 2

If the Angel of the Lord is simply another way of describing the Lord God, why do the two of them seem to be treated as separate individuals? 'The angel is equated with the Lord in some texts and yet appears distinctive in others.'[5]

Those who study ancient messengers acknowledge that someone's envoy could be treated as if he were the authoritative sender. When Joseph's steward confronts Joseph's brothers on their homeward travels, both parties treat the steward as if he were Joseph himself (Gen. 44:9–10). In one of Moses' sermons, he starts speaking about God but then slips into speaking *as* God (Deut. 29:2–4, 5–6). The shift in the sermon is so confronting that some translations, like the updated NIV, introduce a change of speaker by discreetly adding words such as 'Yet the LORD says . . .'; others paraphrase Moses' first-person speech *as* God to third-person words *about* God (e.g. GNB, NIrV, NLT). The same tendency to speak directly on God's behalf can be found in the prophets. Other examples of messengers speaking for and being treated as their senders occur in both the Old and New Testaments (e.g. Judg. 11:12–13; 2 Sam. 3:12–14; 1 Kgs 20:2–4).

This is important when, in both Old Testament Hebrew and New Testament Greek, the word for 'angel' could readily be translated as 'one who is sent with a message'. So perhaps the Angel is God's assigned messenger who, according to the customs of the day, was able to present himself as God and to be treated as God.

Candidate 3

Conservative readers of Scripture, typically under the influence of arguments such as Justin Martyr's, have sought to combine both sets of data observed so far. The Angel sometimes presents as God and is treated like God. At other times the Angel is distinguished from the God from whom he was sent and on whose behalf he speaks.

---

5. Kenneth A. Mathews, *Genesis 11:27–50:26*, NAC 1B (Nashville: B & H, 2005), p. 188. Almost identical language is offered by other authors on other biblical books, e.g. Peter Enns, *Exodus*, NIVAC (Grand Rapids: Zondervan, 2000), p. 96; George L. Klein, *Zechariah*, NAC 21B (Nashville: B & H, 2008), p. 99.

The obvious and orthodox candidate is God the Son. Jesus himself advocates this kind of identity and function, especially in John's Gospel. On the last night of his earthly ministry, the Son confirmed to the Father concerning the disciples, 'I have given them the words that you gave me, and they have received them and have come to know in truth that I came from you; and they have believed that you sent me' (John 17:8 ESV).

Jesus himself acknowledges his task of being sent to speak. Aided by other theological arguments in a similar vein, he becomes a prime candidate for accomplishing the same ministry in the Old Testament. We can appreciate why the preincarnate Son is considered a plausible solution – if not the necessary conclusion – to the identity of the elusive Angel who is simultaneously God and not God.

Summary of candidates

This quick survey shows how each candidate approximates each of the three stages in the syllogism above. Candidate 1 accords with the global recognition that the Angel sounds like he is God. Candidate 2 accounts for the fact that the Angel is sometimes seen as distinct from God even while speaking and being treated as God. Candidate 3 further accommodates both observations, adequately and attractively explaining an agent who is simultaneously God and not God.

Again we can appreciate why the Angel of the Lord is paraded as concrete evidence of christophanies. The two phenomena mutually support each other. The preincarnate Son of God would be the solution to the paradox concerning 'the "angel of the LORD" who is both *identified* as God and yet *differentiated* from God'.[6] In turn the Angel would provide a clear and recurrent example of christophanies.

Of course, various other hypotheses are put forward, exploring how the New Testament descriptions of Jesus might be modelled

---

6. Robert L. Reymond, *A New Systematic Theology of the Christian Faith*, 2nd ed. (Nashville: Thomas Nelson, 2002), p. 208 (italics original). Reymond is another influential scholar who endorses christophanies as 'the teaching of the Old Testament itself' (p. 535).

on the Old Testament Angel – or whether Jesus himself might be some kind of angel. Such hypotheses are intriguing and debatable, but are focused more on New Testament phenomena. My concern is with what is going on in the Old Testament; I will leave further corollaries for others to pursue.

Pronouncing judgment

With three plausible candidates before us, which best explains the details recorded in Scripture? The Angel is somehow related to Old Testament theophanies. Can we further clarify his identity to be the preincarnate Son and thus verify these theophanies to be christophanies?

As we proceed to consider the biblical evidence, it's helpful to review how previous generations have resolved the issue. A brief case history further aids us by showing that different solutions have held sway in different eras and why various supporters (past and present) promote their particular preferences. What we find is that our three candidates have, very roughly, held sway in reverse order.[7]

In due course we'll consider if the New Testament offers any contribution. My opinion is that it does not have any bearing on the identity of the Angel. (The most useful hint, in Acts 7:35, leans toward Candidate 2: the authorized representative of God.) Among the subsequent generation of believers, we've noted that Justin Martyr was an enthusiastic supporter of Candidate 3.

This interpretation – that the Angel was a repeated preincarnate manifestation of the divine Son – held sway for several centuries. Joel

---

7. The history of interpretation can be found in various sources. As well as Walton's summary (n. 3 above), helpful examples include William Graham MacDonald, 'Christology and "The Angel of the Lord"', in Gerald F. Hawthorne (ed.), *Current Issues in Biblical and Patristic Interpretation* (Grand Rapids: Eerdmans, 1975), pp. 324–335; and the dissertation of Joel I. Huffstutler, 'He Who Dwelt in the Bush: A Biblical and Historical Theology of the Angel of the Lord' (PhD diss., Bob Jones University, 2007), pp. 17–61.

Huffstutler outlines several reasons for the popularity of this view, not least as the fledgling Christian movement sought (for various motivations) to show itself as the legitimate extension of Judaism.

Over time the goals, opponents and status of the church changed. From early in the fourth century, Christianity became the official religion of the Roman Empire. Internal debates over the nature of Jesus Christ continued to fester as ever newer generations of believers wrestled with what it meant that he was both fully divine and fully human. Exploring the Trinity, the celebrated church leader and thinker Augustine asked questions about God's invisibility similar to those we considered in part 1. He, however, resolved the question of God's invisibility the opposite way. Not only does John 1:18 nominate God the Father as invisible, but the inclusion of the rest of the Trinity in passages such as the doxologies of 1 Timothy 1:17 and 6:15–16 means that the Son (like the Spirit) is *also* invisible. For Augustine, the Old Testament theophanies and appearances of the Angel could no more be manifestations of the Son than of the Father. So Augustine posited that the Angel was a mere creature, a 'regular' angel sent to do God's bidding and communicate his wishes. Augustine laid the groundwork for Candidate 2, and his view prevailed for more than a millennium.

We celebrate that the sixteenth-century Reformers reclaimed many important truths about Jesus and about the Old Testament. Some of Augustine's teachings were readily promulgated; others were jettisoned. Church thinkers largely returned to the view of the Angel held prior to Augustine, Candidate 3, with the Angel interpreted as the preincarnate Son. The influence of Reformers such as John Calvin and Martin Luther has seen this view upheld in many Protestant circles in the five centuries since. Although perhaps a little eager, Borland is reasonable in claiming that this view he defends is 'the most ancient view of the church', 'the usual conservative biblical position', 'which has the support of most orthodox scholars'.[8]

---

8. Borland, *Christ in the Old Testament*, pp. 58, 59, 55. Borland claims this of christophanies in general, but the identity of the Angel is at the heart of his certainty. This certainty is somewhat undermined when Borland later allows that scholars have not really reached consensus (p. 137).

What we observe in this brief historical survey is that Candidate 1 has not really been given much consideration. The primary positions held throughout church history have been those describing Candidates 2 and 3. As we'll see, the majority of those who investigate the Angel are trying to defend one of these two views and usually target any of their polemic against the other. It's my observation that Candidate 1 is slowly starting to overtake the other two as a viable interpretation. It may eventually become the most agreed consensus. I certainly intend to demonstrate that it's the most sensible and defensible of the three options, even though few in the past have been willing to settle for it.

6. CANDIDATE 1: GOD UNSPECIFIED

As we turn to consider each of the candidates in more detail, I suggest that Candidate 1 may prove to be the Steven Bradbury gold medallist when it comes to identifying the Angel of the Lord. We in sunny Australia were delighted when Bradbury unexpectedly won speed-skating gold at the 2002 Winter Olympics. Trailing towards the back of the pack and without any hope against seasoned competitors from the northern hemisphere, Bradbury's moment came when the leading skaters all collided. Bypassing their tangled bodies, he was effectively the last man standing and the winner of the final.

It seems to me there's insufficient evidence to retain confidence in Candidate 3, the most complex of the three options. Neither is there much evidence for Candidate 2. Candidate 1 thus remains the most likely interpretation. Even if Candidate 2 should struggle across the line, neither Candidate 1 nor Candidate 2 offers the degree of clarity Candidate 3 requires. We can have little confidence that the Angel of the Lord embodies the preincarnate Son. The star example of Old Testament christophanies does not perform.

What we do find, however, is that a Candidate 1 'win' reinforces the findings of part 1. Being unable to reduce the options to the

Son alone, we can and should still affirm that the entire Trinity (or any member thereof, including God the Father) has participated in regular perceivable interactions with God's world and the people made in God's image.

What is universally agreed

We've already observed that all interested parties accept that the Angel is often described as if he were God himself. Among several such summaries, one dictionary captures succinctly the relevant comparisons and texts:

> The deity of this unique angel is suggested by the facts that he (1) is identified as God (Gen 16:7–13; 18:2, 10, 13; 22:10–12, 15–18; Ex 3:2–6, 14, 18; Judg 2:1, 5; 6:11, 14, 16), (2) is recognized as God (Gen 16:9–13; Judg 6:22–24; 13:21–23; cf. Gen 32:24–30 with Hos 12:4–5), (3) is described in terms befitting the Deity alone (Ex 3:2–9, 14; 23:20–23; Josh 5:15), (4) calls himself God (Gen 31:11, 13 [in reference to the 'angel of God']; Ex 3:2, 6, 14), (4) receives worship (Josh 5:14; Judg 2:4–5) and (5) speaks with divine authority (Judg 2:1–5).[1]

Everyone acknowledges that Candidate 1 in the line-up is a viable suspect. The question at stake is whether we can press further and *better* identify one of the remaining candidates.

The quick historical survey showed that nearly twenty centuries of Christian thought have attempted to move beyond Candidate 1 to favour one of the two additional options. Interpreters are either swayed by Augustine or by Justin Martyr and the Reformers. As a result, they quickly accept these agreed observations that the Angel is presented as God but rarely pause to digest the significance of the claims before racing ahead.

There is value in our taking a moment longer to inspect the evidence. There are other arguments that show that 'Angel of the Lord'

---

1. Mark F. Rooker, 'Theophany', in *DOTP*, pp. 863–864 (his square brackets).

may well be another divine title for God. If 'Angel' is used more as a *title* than as a functional *description*, there may be fewer grounds to plough ahead any further and try to discern what kind of 'messenger' is at work. It may well be adequate to accept that the Angel is God without warrant to narrow down his identity more precisely.

What is sometimes debated

Scholars often get hung up on several issues. These are relevant if it's to be resolved that the Angel can be defined more precisely than another title for God. So it's worth rehearsing these because they are sometimes raised when distinguishing Candidates 2 and 3. Again, I would encourage 'settling' for Candidate 1, but it's still helpful to understand the arguments presented in the debate.

What is an 'angel'?

The first issue is what we actually mean or understand by 'angel'. The Hebrew word in the Old Testament (*mal'āk*) refers to any kind of messenger, whether human or supernatural (the kind we traditionally view with wings and optional halo). So already we may misunderstand what's at stake if we hear 'angel' and think 'shiny'. We have to allow that the word applies to a range of figures.

Four times in 2 Samuel 11:18–25 we hear about the messenger (*mal'āk*) who communicates back and forth between King David and his battlefield commander, Joab. A similar concentration is found with three occurrences in 2 Kings 6:32–33. And so it is throughout the Old Testament; estimates suggest that 20–50% of the singular terms describe a human messenger. The plural form (*mal'ākîm*) is even more indicative of this trend; nearly 90% of occurrences denote groups of human messengers.

Although trending more towards our English sense of 'shiny', the same ambivalence is found in the Greek equivalent (*angelos*). When John the Baptist's disciples bring a message to Jesus, they are also described as John's 'angels' (i.e. 'messengers'; Luke 7:18, 24; cf. 9:52). The spies whom Rahab hid are likewise described with this word (Jas 2:25). *Angelos* is used almost exclusively for *mal'āk* in Greek translations of the Old Testament.

Perhaps the most focused and balanced scholar is Samuel Meier. He recognizes the difficulties of finding the right English translation, noting that 'angel' communicates both too narrowly and too broadly.[2] When the identity of a *mal'āk* is unclear, it might be better to avoid the prejudicial translation 'angel'. One recent commentator models this well, starting with the more neutral 'messenger of the Lord' and allowing the wider narrative to clarify anything further.[3]

This forces us to acknowledge that the formal title 'messenger of the Lord/Yahweh' (*mal'ak yhwh*) is not used exclusively of our enigmatic Angel. At least late in the Old Testament the title describes the prophet Haggai and the human priest (Hag. 1:13; Mal. 2:7). Again, there's reason not to race ahead too quickly.

Is there only one, unique 'Angel of the Lord'?

Those who race ahead too quickly can imply or infer that the 'Angel of the Lord' is a title used exclusively of one individual. That would apply particularly well to Candidate 1 (another title for God) and Candidate 3 (seen consistently as the preincarnate Son).

The usage in Haggai and Malachi suggests that we cannot always apply the title to a single individual. This does not favour any of our three candidates. But it does mean we cannot universally see the phrase and interpret our preferred identity. We have to reconsider the phrase on each occasion.

This even suggests that there might be many individuals who can be described as God's messenger. The 'Angel of the Lord' is no more a specific individual than is 'the courier from Australia Post'. There is a generic job description and it's applied to whomever is assigned the task today.

---

2. Samuel A. Meier, 'Angels, Messengers, Heavenly Beings', in Mark J. Boda and J. Gordon McConville (eds.), *Dictionary of the Old Testament: Prophets* (Downers Grove: IVP Academic; Nottingham: Inter-Varsity Press, 2012), pp. 24–25; cf. Meier, *The Messenger in the Ancient Semitic World*, HSM 45 (Atlanta: Scholars Press, 1988); 'Angel I' and 'Angel of Yahweh', in *DDD*, pp. 45–50, 53–59.

3. Barry G. Webb, *The Book of Judges*, NICOT (Grand Rapids: Eerdmans, 2012), e.g. pp. 129–130.

Scholars then get themselves tied in knots trying to determine how much weight might be placed on the notion of *'the* Angel of the Lord'. Those concerned to defend Candidate 3 and christophanies especially are compelled to prove that there's only a single Angel, who keeps appearing throughout the Old Testament. Conversely, if it can be demonstrated that the phrase is indefinite, *'an* angel of the Lord' is likely to be a label designating one of many angels filling that role over time: the description of Candidate 2. Given that these have been the two dominant contenders throughout church history, the debate over 'the' versus 'an' has been incredibly intense.

The debate is unlikely to prove conclusive. The Hebrew phrase simply cannot, on its own, guarantee one reading over the other. There are even options beyond the two that we can express easily in English. Matters get even more complicated when we consider how the phrase is used in the Greek translation of the Old Testament and how the phrase does or does not correspond when it's used in the New Testament.[4]

Without engaging the gruesome grammatical details, the scholarly consensus is that we should probably be consistent between the Old and New Testaments and their respective languages. This bodes badly for Candidate 3. Those who would identify the Angel of the Old Testament with the Jesus of the New Testament must excuse mentions of an 'angel of the Lord' in the New Testament as a different, irregular and irrelevant agent. In terms of English phrases, christophanies require *'the* Angel of the Lord' in Genesis to Malachi but *'an* angel of the Lord' in Matthew to Revelation.

What is often overlooked

We're starting to appreciate that most of the words in the phrase 'the Angel of the Lord' are open to query. It's unclear whether we're

---

4. The issues are introduced completely but concisely by Meier, 'Angel of Yahweh', p. 54.

dealing with a divine angel or a human messenger. It's certainly debated whether there is only one individual sent repeatedly to communicate on God's behalf, or a fleet of couriers scurrying around.

The terms in the latter half of the phrase are seldom considered with nearly such detail or ferocity.

Interpreters usually allow 'the Lord' to mean whatever best fits their understanding. If the Angel is thought to be God the Son, then 'the Lord' (= 'the LORD' = 'Yahweh') is assigned to God the Father. Proponents of the other two candidates are less worried about clarifying the divine name. Interestingly, it's nearly always 'Yahweh' who 'appears' in theophanies.

What is always assumed but rarely explored is the word 'of'. It's actually as important as any other term in the phrase. It may well be the deciding factor, the casting vote that breaks the deadlock. Given its importance and its neglect, we'll spend a few paragraphs thinking it over.

The idea of 'of' is as tricky in English as it is in Hebrew and Greek. When I ask people to name the songs of Michael Jackson, they start listing famous tunes like 'Thriller' or 'Beat It' or 'Billie Jean'. They provide songs *sung by* Michael Jackson. Very, very occasionally someone nominates 'We Are The World' or the sound-track to Sonic the Hedgehog 3: songs *written by* Michael Jackson. No one ever answers 'Eleanor Rigby' or 'Can't Buy Me Love', though, as he has held the copyright to half the Beatles' catalogue for more than a quarter century, these are songs *owned by* Michael Jackson. We could press still further and explore what he kept on his iPod (perhaps some Metallica?) or various tribute tracks about him such as 'Better on the Other Side'. These all qualify as songs *of* Michael Jackson if we pause to consider how versatile that two-letter preposition is.

Interpreters are equally hasty to ignore alternatives for the Angel of the Lord. Because a *mal'āk* is a messenger, the 'of' is regularly assumed to indicate the sender: the Angel *of* the Lord is a messenger *sent by* Yahweh. Walter Kaiser expresses this in one of his earliest descriptions: 'The identity of this particular Angel appears to be more than just an angelic messenger from God . . . He carried an identity with God; yet He was also sent from

Him!'[5] Kaiser clearly counts God and the Angel as two separate individuals, with one sending the other. James Borland even further clarifies both sending and sender: 'Both the Angel of Jehovah and Christ were *sent by the Father*.'[6] The connection is typically treated as cursorily as this.

No matter how sensible this connection might seem, we should investigate whether or not it's correct. It transpires that several other interpretations are equally viable.

It's uncontested that a *mal'āk* is someone sent with a message. The noun is even derived from a verb for sending (*l'k*). The Old Testament attests many dozen examples of a *mal'āk* or *mal'ākîm* being sent. Some of these are even sent by God (e.g. Gen. 24:7, 40).

The question is whether our particular Angel of the Lord fits the mould of other such messengers. For a start, we never read a phrase such as 'God *sent* the Angel of the Lord'. Granted, there are mentions of God's sending 'his angel' or 'my angel', but interpreters merely assume that this refers to the 'Angel of the Lord' because of their assumptions about 'of'. It remains to be seen that these various phrases all describe the one figure. Moreover, Meier's study of the Angel begins by observing that this particular *mal'āk* does not follow the behaviour of other such figures in the ancient world; Meier warns us not to transfer in simplistic fashion what we know about other messengers and angels.[7]

Few scholars investigate the relationship between the two titles 'Angel' and 'Lord'. When they do, they usually conclude that we're dealing with a very special sense of the connecting 'of'. Although it won't work for 'the songs of Michael Jackson', an 'of' can behave

---

5. Walter C. Kaiser Jr., *Toward an Old Testament Theology* (Grand Rapids: Zondervan, 1978), p. 85. Having defined the Angel this way, Kaiser's next sentence uses the term 'christophany'. The same language persists in Kaiser's *The Promise-Plan of God* (Grand Rapids: Zondervan, 2008), p. 53.

6. James A. Borland, *Christ in the Old Testament*, 2nd ed. (Fearn: Mentor, 1999), p. 62 (italics original).

7. Meier, 'Angel of Yahweh', p. 53 (partly cited in chapter 7 of this book).

as an equals sign and be translated something like 'i.e.' or 'that is'. There are at least three reasons for thinking this likely here. The first is that there are other constructions like this in Hebrew. Especially in the books of Isaiah and Lamentations we find the populace of a city described as the 'daughter of' that city. To choose a familiar example, reprised in the New Testament in John 12:15, consider the following translations of Zechariah 9:9:

> Rejoice greatly, O daughter of Zion!
>   Shout aloud, O daughter of Jerusalem!
> (ESV; cf. NASB)

> Rejoice greatly, O daughter Zion!
>   Shout aloud, O daughter Jerusalem!
> (NRSV; cf. NIV, HCSB)

In each line, how many individuals are envisioned? Does Zechariah address a daughter who is distinct from Zion/Jerusalem? That is the implication of the former, more rigid, translation. But the latter translation captures more accurately the sense that the daughter personifies the city; there is an additional, evocative label that further describes the *one* entity.[8]

The same is found with other nouns followed by 'of' and then a name. The most obvious of these would rigidly be translated 'the river *of* Euphrates', but even the literalistic versions above recognize that it means 'the river *that is* Euphrates' and simply translate as 'the river Euphrates'. Douglas Stuart observes this in his commentary on Exodus and argues that this is how we should understand the Angel of the Lord. The phrase means 'the angel *that is* Yahweh' and might even be translated as 'Angel Yahweh'. It's hardly a new

---

8. William F. Stinespring, 'No Daughter of Zion: A Study of the Appositional Genitive in Hebrew Grammar', *Enc* 26 (1965), e.g. p. 135. Stinespring, citing Ps. 9:14 ('the gates of Daughter Zion') and Lam. 2:8 ('the wall around Daughter Zion'), further argues we should not consider 'daughter' to refer to the population but to the city itself.

idea, with traces of this same solution found at least as far as two centuries back.[9]

Another reason for pursuing this identification is that the Bible seems attached to the full title. If the phrase means an 'angel sent by the Lord', we might expect subsequent mentions within the same story to refer back to 'the angel' already introduced. We would not need to keep hearing who had sent him. But the Bible almost invariably repeats the full title, as if mention of 'Lord' is just as important as 'angel'. We see this in the first Angel of the Lord encounter in Genesis 16:7–14; the full phrase occurs four times, whenever the Angel of the Lord is mentioned. We find ten occurrences of the title in fourteen verses when the Angel of the Lord encounters Balaam (Num. 22:22–35) and five occurrences in three verses concerning Gideon (Judg. 6:20–22).

A third reason is widely recognized. Biblical texts commonly interchange 'Angel of the Lord' with 'Lord' or 'God'. Christophany proponents regularly defend this idea that the Angel is presented *as* God.

Other reasons for equating the Angel and God could be explored, though they are inconclusive. For example, although the Angel behaves and speaks as God, he never describes himself as an angel or messenger. We might expect that if he were a mere envoy. The Angel does not describe himself in any way, so we're left to guess at this silence. And, in addition to the observations about the sense of 'of', it's possible that the phrase never conveyed the 'of' at all. It all depends on how the extra squiggles that represent Hebrew vowels are interpreted. These are often considered to be later additions to the inspired consonantal text, so the original wording may always have described a single figure: 'the Angel, Yahweh'. Finally, and perhaps a little more persuasively (though still an argument from silence), there does not seem to be *any* example of the singular

---

9. Douglas K. Stuart, *Exodus*, NAC 2 (Nashville: B & H, 2006), pp. 110–111, citing Stinespring and several other Hebrew studies. Such grammar is accepted by Timothy Dwight, *Theology, Explained and Defended, in a Series of Sermons* (London: Baynes & Son, 1818), vol. 2, p. 69, though he thinks both terms describe the Son.

phrase 'messenger of X'. Although it's common to construe our Angel as a 'messenger *sent by* God', we do not actually find corresponding examples such as 'an envoy of Solomon' or 'an ambassador of Hezekiah' using the word *mal'āk*.

To summarize, there's every reason to accept the arguments that the Angel of the Lord is some kind of appearance of God himself. Again, those who want the Angel to be the preincarnate Son (Candidate 3) work hard at showing this; we should accept their evidence. And those who allow that a messenger represents his sender (Candidate 2) also admit that the Angel is cast as indistinguishable from his sender. This chapter has furnished additional reasons for identifying the Angel and God. The evidence for the base case (Candidate 1) is even stronger than usually recognized.

What difficulties remain?

Of course things are not quite as tidy as this. If there were conclusive knockdown arguments, there would not be ongoing debate about the Angel's identity. So it's worth recognizing that one or two difficulties persist with accepting Candidate 1.

One issue is why the Angel speaks about God as if God were someone else. When we explore this topic in the next chapter, we'll find there are plausible reasons why one might refer to oneself in the third person.

In turn, this asks why use the label 'Angel of the Lord' at all. There are already several other divine names or titles, such as 'Yahweh/Lord', various words for 'God', another for 'Lord', and so on. What are the biblical authors – and perhaps God himself – aiming to achieve by having him appear and being described as an angel or messenger? At the very least, we ought not to baulk at the possibility of another title or name for God; plenty of others are accepted. Bible readers usually don't blink when a passage employs several of these in quick succession. It's simply because church history has taught us to think of the Angel of the Lord as a separate, sent individual that we don't naturally treat this as another synonym for God. Yet an inspection of the biblical text tends to encourage us to interpret the title 'Angel of the Lord' as another divine name.

The interaction between the Angel and Gideon in Judges 6 illustrates this well. Not only do we find that titles such as 'Yahweh' and 'God' and 'Sovereign' are readily substituted for each other, but it makes the story run as smoothly as possible if 'Angel of the Lord' is also another title for God. It does not iron out all the kinks in the story-telling and Gideon clearly does not understand a lot of what is going on, but it minimizes the jarring if the Angel and God are conflated.

Some protest that God is not otherwise called an 'angel'. That is a difficult argument to evaluate on its own, especially if we do resolve that the various appearances of the 'Angel of the Lord' qualify as appearances of God – and when christophany proponents insist that we identify God the Son as this 'Angel'. The general issues surrounding the word *mal'āk* recur when it appears twice in Malachi 3:1, complicated because the verse is used in the New Testament to talk about John the Baptist's preparing the way for Jesus. One mention occurs in a unique title, 'the messenger of the covenant'. While opinions vary wildly, I think the most sensible reading of the verse and the phrase has this describing God himself (and not, as some would have it, Jesus in particular or some other angel). If so, we do find an additional instance of God's willingly calling himself a *mal'āk*.[10]

The example of Gideon and others like it help us begin to see why God might allow and use the guise of a messenger. These are occasions when God wants to walk among his people and com-municate with them, yet in a fairly incognito fashion. We are back to the *Prince and the Pauper* scenario, with a monarch moving among his people without immediately being recognized. The consistent pattern is that, if the Angel of the Lord is formally identified by his human interlocutors at all, it's not until the end of their encounter. He is usually indistinguishable from any other man, with nothing at all 'angelic' about him. Although the realization shocks those who have encountered and survived God, it ought not to surprise us. Especially in the light of Jesus' incarnation we know that God seeks to live among his people and interact with them. We know he

---

10. I outline the issues and my conclusions in 'Is the Messiah Announced in Malachi 3:1?', *TynB* 57 (2006), pp. 215–228.

accommodates himself to that particular, unique theophany. Even before the incarnation God accommodated himself in non-human forms so that he might lead the exodus generation in a pillar of cloud and fire and a cloud of glory. His presence was somehow more concentrated in the midst of the Israelites and even more concentrated again in the Most Holy Place and around the ark of the covenant. Even though the fullness of deity dwelt in the incarnate Jesus, this revelation was not so complete that the entire world recognized God. As we saw in part 1, the New Testament itself admits that Jesus was a muted theophany. Even though we don't know how God effects a theophany, or even precisely why, we know he is in the habit of toning down his full glory in order to spend time among his people. It may even be that appearances of the Angel of the Lord were part of God's educational programme to prepare people for his more substantial and significant appearance in the incarnation.[11]

Where are we up to?

So far we have been working through the evidence that closely aligns the Angel of the Lord with God himself. Again, the case for Candidate 1 is hardly contentious for orthodox Christians. The question is whether we can sufficiently *distinguish* the Angel from God so that we can further identify him as a creaturely agent sent on God's behalf (Candidate 2) or even as the divine Son (Candidate 3). We consider each of those in the coming chapters.

As we do, it's important to remember two things. First, the evidence for and implications of Candidate 1 are often given short shrift. Because the history of interpretation has focused only on Candidates 2 and 3, proponents of each of those positions tend to train their combative sights against the other. Proponents of each position – who comprise the bulk of scholars investigating the Angel

---

11. These ideas are sometimes surveyed in studies of the Angel. Some here are developed from the remainder of Stuart's excursus, *Exodus*, pp. 112–113.

– tend to lump Candidate 1 in with their opponents and unnecessarily discard this option. We've already encountered Joel Huffstutler as he attempts to defend Candidate 3 and thus christophanies. For him, the Angel is either Jesus or some creaturely agent; there's no middle ground between these 'two primary views'.[12] Shortly we'll meet René López, a recent champion of Candidate 2. He similarly presupposes that any arguments favouring Candidate 1 are attempts to endorse Candidate 3 (as they often are) and discards the two views concurrently. We might tweak the familiar axiom and suggest that López assumes 'any friend of my enemy is also my enemy'.

The second thing to remember is that it's Candidate 3 who is of relevance to the question of Old Testament christophanies. Demonstrating that the Angel is God (Candidate 1) only affirms theophanies in general, not christophanies in particular. If we should determine that the Angel is a commissioned agent (Candidate 2), we certainly have strong evidence against the possibility of christophanies. Those keen to identify christophanies must be willing to accept at least the evidence presented so far. The question is whether there's sufficient evidence to refine further the identity of the Angel from being God in general to being the divine Son in particular.

---

12. The polarization between two views is found from the start of his first chapter through to his last appendix: Joel I. Huffstutler, 'He Who Dwelt in the Bush: A Biblical and Historical Theology of the Angel of the Lord' (PhD diss., Bob Jones University, 2007), pp. 17, 286.

7. CANDIDATE 2: A MUNDANE MESSENGER

Interpreters explore a solution beyond the one we've reached so far because there are times when the Angel appears to be distinct from God, as history has also taught us to presume. This generates the tension concerning the Angel: he seems to alternate between being God and being not God.

The solution we've already surveyed (Candidate 1) emphasizes how Angel and God are all but indistinguishable. Various interpreters have been unhappy with the Angel's being God and have proposed the second solution (Candidate 2), which accommodates the fact that the two do sometimes seem to be separate. The crucial advancement has been to explain why a separate messenger can still speak and act and be treated as if he were God. But this advancement has overlooked other impediments to the 'messenger solution'.

Does this work?

We've already glimpsed the grounds on which Candidate 2 is often explained, particularly among recent interpreters. There's evidence that you would treat a messenger as you would treat the one who sent him. I've mentioned some of the Old Testament examples of this. The same sentiment is expressed in the New Testament. Jesus attests that the treatment of his disciples reflects a reaction to him, just as someone's response to Jesus is a response to God the Father (e.g. Matt. 10:40).[1]

Various details of this messenger solution to the Angel's identity might be challenged. This is the domain of specialists such as Samuel Meier. For example, he observes that messengers still identify themselves as messengers, even if they then speak as their sender. If so, our confidence in Candidate 2 diminishes when the Angel fails to introduce himself.[2]

Among such details, I wish to challenge two in particular. I single these out because they have not received adequate attention in explorations of the Angel's identity. More importantly, the two issues are foundational to claims for Candidate 2. These may not be final nails in the coffin, but they underscore assumptions that need to be further tested before we can pronounce with any confidence that the Angel is an individual distinct from God.

Challenge 1: Do narrators distinguish the Angel from God?

Whether with twins at church or quins in *The Five Chinese Brothers*, the challenge is how to tell them apart. Confusion escalates only when there are difficulties with differentiation. I am grateful half the pairs of twins at church are not completely identical; one or two

---

1. Among scholars already mentioned, Candidate 2 is favoured by the likes of William Graham MacDonald, 'Christology and "The Angel of the Lord"', in Gerald F. Hawthorne (ed.), *Current Issues in Biblical and Patristic Interpretation* (Grand Rapids: Eerdmans, 1975), pp. 331–332; and John H. Walton, *Genesis*, NIVAC (Grand Rapids: Zondervan, 2001), pp. 464–466. See now René A. López, 'Identifying the "Angel of the Lord" in the Book of Judges: A Model for Reconsidering the Referent in Other Old Testament Loci', *BBR* 20 (2010), pp. 1–18.

2. Samuel A. Meier, 'Angel I' and 'Angel of Yahweh', in *DDD*, pp. 49, 58.

pairs vary in face shape, one pair differs in hair colour (literally black versus white!) and a couple of pairs comprise girl and boy. It's the remaining, identical pairs that create most difficulty.

We need to ask on what grounds we can distinguish the Angel from God. If we're confident we're dealing with separate individuals, *then* we need to explain why the Angel can speak and act and be treated like God. But it's futile to marshal evidence for the 'messenger solution' if it does not apply in this situation. There may be good answers, but it's unclear if there is a question to address. (Preachers sometimes lament that they have an excellent illustration and just need to find the right passage from which to preach it!)

As I eagerly digested the promising presentation of René López, I found a simple and surprising problem. The Angel debate has always oscillated between Candidates 3 and 2: proponents of either identity have not given due consideration to Candidate 1. Moreover, even though proponents for both traditional options are firmly entrenched against each other, both are guilty of the same, flawed methodology. Both focus virtually all their energies on the *similarities* between the Angel and God, either to show the Angel as divine or as a closely identified and authorized representative. Neither faction has given very much attention to what *differentiates* the Angel and God.

Yet this is a crucial issue when identifying the Angel. There is no problem for Candidate 1; everyone recognizes the overlap. Supporters of Candidate 2 need to establish *that* we're dealing with a messenger who looks, sounds and acts like his superior, not merely *how* this would work. As we'll see in the next chapter, those voting for Candidate 3 have to balance both factors with unbelievable precision. Identifying the Angel as the divine Son – simultaneously God and not God – requires a demonstration of *both* the similarities *and* the differences.

Throughout history there has been inadequate contemplation of this simple, central question. What distinguishes the Angel from God?

Several possible answers can be offered. They are not particularly compelling. They could prove true if we were already convinced of one of the historical options, but they don't require either option to be true. They don't arbitrate between these two popular factions and are usually just assumed without further inspection. We attempt that inspection now as we consider the possible ways the Angel might be distinguished from God.[3]

Different labels

The very first difference is their labelling. One is called the 'Angel of the Lord', while the other is named 'the Lord' or 'God'. That's a valid observation. From Genesis to Malachi inspired authors have chosen this phrase when there are plenty of other titles. They give every impression they are narrating a separate individual such as a 'prophet of the Lord' or a 'man of God'.

On the one hand, this is an important observation. We're familiar with messengers being distinct from their senders. God sends various messengers and angels. So there could well be a sense here of one (or more) of God's underlings at work as God communicates with his world.

On the other hand, the label 'Angel of the Lord' is not conclusive. We've learned just how much this Angel is described almost identically with God. The label could denote the 'Angel *who is* the Lord'. We never meet a singular 'messenger of Nebuchadnezzar'. We never find the fully titled 'Angel of the Lord' being sent. Just as 'Angel of the Lord' is assumed to be a title of a separate individual, it could just as readily be another divine title for God himself.

One possible reason for this title is that reverent Jewish authors or scribes sometimes avoided naming or describing God directly; perhaps they have politely conjured up an acceptable alter ego. Or it may be that 'Angel' helpfully depicts the guise in which God tones himself down for interacting with humans; the 'Angel of the Lord' is God's undercover alias. These suggestions are plausible, though they can get quite complex when investigated further. Does the alias originate with God or with his narrators? Why is the codename employed on some occasions but not others? Nonetheless, when it's employed, the title works well as an alternative name for God without having to propose a separate individual working on his behalf.

---

3. These chapters are developed from my article 'Distinguishing the Angel of the Lord', *BBR* 21 (2011), pp. 297–314, a response to López.

So the two different labels can be explained in two different ways. The existence of the phrase does not in itself favour one interpretation or another.

Different appearances

Scholars sometimes indeed hint that the Angel is a kind of disguise for God, either to protect God from being recognized or to protect the humans he encounters from the danger of his raw visage. Those who champion Candidates 2 and 3 go further, arguing that the Angel is God's regular courier agent, a separate messenger commissioned to interact more visibly or more safely with humanity.

The trouble is that we can have no certainty in this approach. Some of the evidence has already been raised. First, the biblical authors are not consistently concerned to preserve a distinction between God and his agent. The biblical text itself regularly records that 'God' appeared or spoke to many people. If it was God's *agent* who facilitated such transactions, biblical narrators have become a bit slack in preserving the fact. Proponents tell us that this is simply because representatives were *so* common that the distinction didn't need to be underscored continually. This may be true, but it raises further problems to which we'll return.

Secondly, scholars end up tripping over themselves to try to discern which of God's agents are safe to encounter and which are not. Charles Gieschen distinguishes between God's 'glory' and his 'face', judging the former safe and the latter unbearable.[4] Gieschen faces the problem that the two terms are regularly synonymous. His conclusions are also simplistic: we've seen passages where God's glory is no more bearable than God himself (Exod. 33:18–23; 40:34–35; 1 Kgs 8:10–11; Ezek. 1:28). Likewise with the Angel. If he is the safer representative delegate from God, it sounds like special pleading when interpreters simultaneously allow 'how overwhelming and even fatal it can be to see Him in His great glory'.[5]

---

4. Charles A. Gieschen, *Angelomorphic Christology: Antecedents and Early Evidence*, AGJU 42 (Leiden: Brill, 1998), pp. 78–88.

5. Paul Blackham, *A Study Guide to the Book of Exodus* (Carlisle: Authentic Lifestyle, 2003), p. 8.

This leads to a third reason why I'm unconvinced that the Angel is God's distinct messenger. Apart from inconsistencies in scholars' presentations, we find inconsistencies in the application of the theory. If the Angel is God's envoy, why do both Moses and Gideon panic when they encounter this Angel (Exod. 3:1–6; Judg. 6:20–22)? They exhibit a poor grasp of the messenger conventions that were supposedly commonplace.

Different actions

If the Angel were God's envoy, we might expect to find the two of them interacting. In particular, we might expect mention of God's sending the Sent One of the Lord. This is, after all, the definition provided by proponents.

We've already noted that this exact formula is not found in Scripture. There is no passage confirming 'God sent the Angel of the Lord.'

It's true that there are passages where God sends 'his angel' (Gen. 24:7, 40; Dan. 3:28; 6:22) or describes himself as sending 'my angel' (Exod. 23:23; 32:34; Isa. 42:19; Mal. 1:1; 3:1). For anyone presuming that the 'Angel *of* the Lord' describes an 'Angel *controlled by* the Lord' these verses fill the gap and offer attractive evidence. Yet it seems to me that the burden of proof remains with those who would equate these various angels. To see 'my/his angel' as the 'Angel of the Lord' again presupposes, without adequate investigation, what 'of' means. It's unclear that every angel God sends qualifies as the Angel of the Lord (whom God does not overtly send) and it's transparent that several do not (e.g. Isa. 42:19; Mal. 3:1). Some of these angels are sufficiently difficult that scholars who otherwise exalt the Angel excuse them as irrelevant exceptions.[6] Indeed, Bible translations that religiously capitalize 'Angel (of the Lord)' as a sign of deity do not do so with these; the NKJV capitalizes in only two of the nine verses listed, and the newer HCSB *none* of them.

---

6. E.g. John C. Ellis, 'The Angel of the LORD in Genesis and Exodus' (MTh diss., Presbyterian Theological College; Australian College of Theology, 1989), pp. 11, 129.

We may also note that 'sending' something does not prove it to be completely distinct. In many passages, God 'sends' his hand to achieve a task. Although there may be a conceptual difference between God and his hand, they are not substantially disjoint individuals. Of course, one can 'send' someone who *is* distinct, and this remains the natural sense of the verb. But the verb alone does not guarantee individuation.

Further, I'll elaborate shortly just how informative it is when parallel accounts exist. Bible readers are familiar with the overlap between the Gospels of Matthew, Mark and Luke (and, to a lesser degree, John). The most obvious Old Testament overlap occurs when the books of Samuel and Kings are reprised in Chronicles. There is one passage where the later interpretation by Chronicles sheds light on the sending of angels. Near the end of his life, King David is offered a choice between three forms of punishment for a particular sin. David chooses the option most visibly under God's control: three days of plague. The plague climaxes as it's about to consume Jerusalem. That climax is described as an angel's sending forth his hand (2 Sam. 24:16). Already this illustrates that the one who sends and what is sent do not have to be entirely disjoint. In the later retelling, Chronicles uses exactly the same language to describe the plague's climaxing as God's sending forth an angel (1 Chr. 21:15). If the two versions are mutually interpretative, we further find (1) an act of sending between God and angel that may not necessarily distinguish two completely separate individuals, and (2) that the author of Chronicles is content on this occasion to ascribe the actions of the angel in Samuel to God. From the Chronicler's perspective, we get the impression that the angel is an 'appendage', which, like a hand, God sends forth. Indeed, on both occasions, David sees the afflictions caused by the *angel* and begs God to redirect 'your *hand*'.

At this event, God speaks to the angel causing such afflictions. This more clearly intimates a distinction between the two. Note, though, that it's far from certain that we're witnessing the 'Angel of the Lord', and I've been careful not to capitalize 'angel'. Although the fuller phrase does occur here, it may well simply be clarifying an indefinite angel already under discussion. (Again, where the HCSB and NKJV regularly capitalize 'Angel of the Lord' they don't do so here.) Nonetheless, we'll see shortly that God speaks to the (capitalized) Angel on one other occasion.

When such parallels occur elsewhere, they tend to *conflate* the Angel further with God. Interpreters recognize these important passages. At the end of his life, Jacob blesses his grandchildren in the name of 'God . . . God . . . the Angel' (Gen. 48:15–16). It's not strictly the 'Angel of the Lord' but, tellingly, many English translations – that would not otherwise do so – capitalize 'Angel' here (NIV, NLT, AV/KJV, NET, NAB, NCV); several reputable translation teams have determined that the word *mal'āk* can be applied directly to God! When the prophet Hosea recounts Jacob's story, he parallels how Jacob 'struggled with God, struggled with an angel' and then identifies this figure as 'Yahweh, the God of hosts, Yahweh' (Hos. 12:3–5). And where Chronicles describes David as meeting the 'Angel of the Lord' who plagues Jerusalem, the narrator later considers David to have encountered Yahweh himself (2 Chr. 3:1).

The same conflation is found even within single accounts. In the original record of Jacob's struggle by the Jabbok River, his midnight assailant is at first described as 'a man', a man whom most accept as an/the angel and who later concedes that Jacob has 'struggled with God'. Jacob even names the place 'face of God' because he recognizes he has encountered God personally (Gen. 32:22–32). An independent statement elsewhere likewise treats the titles 'God' and 'Angel of the Lord' as synonyms (Zech. 12:8).

I've not addressed every possibility or probability here. Yet it's significant that the Angel is not nearly as distinct from God as is often assumed. Indeed, when parallel accounts offer additional clarification they tend to close the gap between the Angel and God and minimize any difference.

Challenge 2: Does the Angel distinguish himself from God?

Another basis on which the Angel and God are thought to be distinguished is that the Angel speaks to God and about God as if God were someone else. We'll treat this phenomenon separately because it's often presented as the primary evidence for telling the two apart. We'll explore below the different kinds of speaking in turn.

The Angel speaks to God

The first version of this phenomenon is the most persuasive. If we can find the Angel and God speaking to each other, we have good grounds for considering them to be separate individuals. We do indeed find this – to an extremely limited extent.

Interpreters sometimes give the impression that there are regular conversations between the Angel and God. But there's only one instance where we can claim this with any confidence. The other possible occasion is the one already considered, when God appears to command the angel to stop plaguing Jerusalem as punishment for David's census. But it's not clear whether that angel is distinct from God, or even whether he qualifies as the formal 'Angel of the Lord'.

The one undisputed instance occurs in Zechariah 1:7–17. Old Testament scholars regularly wrestle with how to count and identify the various individuals narrated. Most agree there is a 'man' and an 'angel', and that the sudden mention of the 'Angel of the Lord' is a fresh description for one of the two figures already introduced (most commonly the man). Regardless of who is who, the Angel of the Lord addresses the Lord in 1:12. Even scholars who might prefer elsewhere to conflate the Angel and God recognize that here there's a distinction drawn between them.

It may be that this is sufficient proof of some sort of distinction between the Angel and God all the way through the Old Testament. If so, we're justified in moving beyond Candidate 1 to consider Candidates 2 and 3. Fans of these latter possibilities need to keep Zechariah 1:12 at the forefront of their arsenal.

The verse does, however, raise a trickier question that some conservative scholars might rather not face. There's the distinct possibility that the label 'Angel of the Lord' cannot be interpreted consistently throughout the Old Testament. The idea is not as shocking as it may sound, but we ought to unpack it gently.

Those who favour Candidate 3 – that the Angel constitutes pre-incarnate appearances of the Son – already allow for a change between the two testaments. The New Testament's 'angel of the Lord' must clearly describe someone different to the Old Testament's 'Angel of the Lord'. We've also acknowledged that some of the Old Testament uses describe human prophetic messengers rather than any divine figure (esp. Hag. 1:13; Mal. 2:7). So it's already accepted that we cannot make a blanket application of the title. Thoughtful conservatives usually concede this point.[7]

We noticed earlier that a rigorous investigation should scrutinize each Angel passage separately. In practice, most interpreters choose their preferred position and alter it only when necessary. This can create a painful collision between competing values: the need for responsible exegetical flexibility and the inertia of an established dogmatic stance. Few of us are exempt from this tension. I'm aware of my preference for Candidate 1 and the internal resistance I experience when Zechariah 1:12 or Haggai 1:13 or Malachi 2:7 each demonstrates that 'Angel of the Lord' cannot universally be another divine title.

For myself, I'm willing to struggle against the preference to determine a single identity of the Angel throughout the Old Testament. One plausible explanation is that Jewish theology matured and even changed (within certain limits) as the Old Testament unfolded. We accept this for Christian theology: the events surrounding Jesus were reflected upon by his apostles and refined by subsequent generations of believers. Several major doctrines, and especially those concerning the Trinity, took several centuries to be distilled into the formulations we take for granted today.

The passages that challenge Candidate 1 and the Angel's complete identification with God all come from the latest books of the Old Testament: Haggai, Zechariah and Malachi. (In the composition of the Old Testament, Chronicles is also a late book. It's actually placed last in the Hebrew Bible.) This accords well with studies that confirm a progressive development in the Jewish understanding of angels in general and of one angel who particularly served as God's chief vizier. Such developments especially occurred in the time between the testaments.[8] So it's suggestive that the latest books in the Old

---

7. E.g. Herman Bavinck, *The Doctrine of God* (Grand Rapids: Eerdmans, 1951), pp. 256–258. Bavinck claims such flexibility can also be found in the famed Reformers Luther and Calvin.

8. E.g. Larry W. Hurtado, *One God, One Lord*, 2nd ed. (Edinburgh: T & T Clark, 1998), pp. 71–92; *Lord Jesus Christ* (Grand Rapids: Eerdmans, 2003), pp. 29–48; Camilla Hélena von Heijne, *The Messenger of the Lord in Early Jewish Interpretation of Genesis* (Berlin: de Gruyter, 2010).

Testament evince most interest in distinguishing the Angel from God; perhaps we're observing the beginnings of the trend that would flourish in the intertestamental period. Earlier Jewish thinkers might have been happier with an interpretation akin to Candidate 1 but progressively clarified their descriptions to sound more like Candidate 2. We certainly see the Candidate 2 approach by the time the New Testament opens.

If Jewish thinking matured over time, we ought to be even less dogmatic about seeking a single interpretation at every point in Scripture. Interestingly, proponents of Candidate 3 accept something of this approach. One of Walter Kaiser's paragraphs concludes, 'One thing for sure, He was not the invisible God. And He acted and talked as the Lord. There the matter apparently rested until revelation clarified the enigma.'[9] Whether or not we accept all of Kaiser's interpretative steps and his own tendency to assume a single identity for the Angel, he allows that readers who had only the Old Testament would not be able to articulate a complete doctrine of that identity. Further revelation was required over a period of time and beyond the Old Testament.

Moreover, responsible exegesis urges us to consider each passage on its own merits. If the later biblical authors painted the Angel in such pallid colours so that he would not be mistaken as a divine rival for Yahweh, we *contravene* their intentions if we strive here to identify the Angel as God in general or the Son in particular! The 'Angel of the Lord' may be identified as Candidate 1 in the earlier books of the Old Testament and as Candidate 2 in the later ones.

We'll also see later that accepting an evolution in the Angel's identity is still a long way from demonstrating that the Angel of the Lord was the preincarnate Son. Several steps need to be established beyond the observation that the Angel was distinct from God. But we've not yet finished establishing whether the Angel can be distinguished from God at all.

---

9. Walter C. Kaiser Jr., *Toward an Old Testament Theology* (Grand Rapids: Zondervan, 1978), p. 85; cf. Derek Kidner, *Genesis*, TOTC 1 (Leicester: Inter-Varsity Press, 1967), pp. 33–34.

The Angel speaks about God

Whether we move as far as Candidate 3, it's still difficult to demonstrate that the Angel is distinct from God. That the Angel addresses God in Zechariah 1:12 is the only concrete suggestion the Old Testament offers even in favour of Candidate 2.

Interpreters recurrently propose one more line of evidence. They find passages where the Angel appears to speak about God as if God were some third party. Modern authors place most – if not all – of their interpretative eggs in this particular basket. We must not underestimate the amount of weight placed upon this argument. Consider the following examples:

> The title Angel of the Lord is particularly striking because it is used in many of these passages interchangeably with the terms Yahweh (Jehovah) and God in such a way as to leave little doubt that the angel is a manifestation of God himself. Nevertheless, at the same time the angel and God clearly are not equated because the angel often refers to God in the third person.[10]

> The biblical theological data of Genesis demonstrates that the Angel of Yahweh is indeed the God of the patriarchs ... At the same time, the biblical data of Genesis indicates that the Angel of Yahweh is in some way distinct from God, because he speaks in [the] third person of Yahweh and God.[11]

We can find the same elsewhere, such as in the writings of Martin Luther.

If the Angel and God are distinct, then of course the Angel can speak about God in the third person. Yet it's fallacious to reverse this. The existence of third-person language does not guarantee separate individuals. That is because individuals can use third-person language to describe themselves. Even a moment's reflection

---

10. J. Robert Vannoy, 'Theophany', in Walter A. Elwell (ed.), *Baker Encyclopedia of the Bible* (Grand Rapids: Baker, 1988), vol. 2, p. 2051.
11. Joel I. Huffstutler, 'He Who Dwelt in the Bush' (PhD diss., Bob Jones University, 2007), p. 102; cf. pp. 74, 77, 95–96, 210, 264; and much of Walton's excursus, *Genesis*, pp. 462–466.

demonstrates this to be true, both in our own contemporary culture and in the cultures of the Old and New Testaments.

I've explored this phenomenon in detail elsewhere.[12] Perhaps the most convincing example is Jesus' prayer the night before his crucifixion, which begins:

> Glorify your Son, that your Son may glorify you. For you granted him authority over all people that he might give eternal life to all those you have given him. Now this is eternal life: that they know you, the only true God, and Jesus Christ, whom you have sent.
> (John 17:1–3)

No one would suggest that Jesus' third-person mentions of 'your Son . . . your Son . . . him . . . he . . . him . . . Jesus Christ' refer to another Son or another Jesus Christ!

Likewise, that the Angel mentions 'the Lord' or 'God' is inconclusive as to whether he is referencing himself or someone else. We can certainly take various factors into account, but this factor alone is insufficient.

Given that I favour Candidate 1 and its thesis that 'Angel of the Lord' is another way to describe God, it is useful to observe that God is as prone as anyone else to refer to himself in such third-person fashion. Many small examples can be found (e.g. Gen. 9:6, 16; Num. 32:11–12; Deut. 1:36). Several others are sometimes thought to give hints of the Trinity, where God seems to speak about another God (esp. Exod. 33:19; 2 Sam. 7:11; Hos. 1:7; Amos 4:11; Zech. 1:17; Mal. 3:1). Each of these can be explained on other grounds, leaving us with the observation that God can mention 'God' without identifying some separate individual.[13]

---

12. Andrew S. Malone, 'God the Illeist: Third-Person Self-References and Trinitarian Hints in the Old Testament', *JETS* 52 (2009), pp. 499–518. 'Illeism' is a formal term for referring to oneself in the third person. Although Samuel Taylor Coleridge coined the term in 1809, the phenomenon can be traced back for millennia.

13. Ibid., esp. pp. 508–513. Reaching the same conclusion, quite independently, see Günther H. Juncker, 'Jesus and the Angel of

It's particularly telling when champions of Candidate 3 acknowledge the phenomenon as they wrestle with the data. We've seen some, such as Huffstutler (at n. 11 above), predicate their entire argument on third-person references as distinguishing the Angel from God. Yet they occasionally abandon the principle when it threatens to undermine their position; it suddenly becomes permissible to allow third-person language as *self*-reference.[14] Indeed, many proponents tacitly allow such language. They often want to see the Lord God who confronts Adam and Eve in the garden as a christophany (Gen. 3:8) and have him then describe the coming Messiah in third-person terms (3:15).[15]

So, again, it would be entirely consistent if the Angel were God and alternated between speaking *as* God and speaking *about* God. We cannot press this consistency so far as to make it further *proof* of the Angel's identity as Candidate 1 (i.e. God). But neither does the phenomenon of the Angel talking about God constitute evidence for Candidate 2 (a distinct messenger) or Candidate 3 (a distinct person of the Trinity, Jesus).

Challenge 3: Should we be able to distinguish the Angel?

These two focused challenges lead to a third broad query about distinguishing the Angel as a messenger separate from God. We can approach this through three complementary issues.

---

the Lord' (PhD diss., Trinity Evangelical Divinity School, 2001), pp. 38–41; and earlier observations by Donald J. Slager, 'Who Is the "Angel of the Lord"?', *BT* 39 (1988), p. 437; Gleason L. Archer Jr., *A Survey of Old Testament Introduction*, 3rd ed. (Chicago: Moody, 1994), p. 488.

14. Huffstutler, 'He Who Dwelt in the Bush', p. 151, n. 32; Ellis, 'Angel of the LORD', p. 114, n. 315; p. 155, n. 431. The same can even be shown for Justin Martyr.

15. Cf. Jonathan Stephen, *Theophany: Close encounters with the Son of God* (Epsom: Day One, 1998), p. 29 and n. 6.

The (ir)relevance of ancient messengers

While the Angel of the Lord sometimes talks about God, he mostly speaks *as* God. This is what raises the question of the Angel's identity in the first place and what proponents of Candidates 2 and 3 seek to accommodate.

Scholars such as René López make a sterling attempt to explain how a messenger in the ancient world could speak and be treated like his master. López rightly rehearses the biblical examples we've already seen, as well as other useful instances we'll meet soon. He even acknowledges the important contributions of Samuel Meier to the topic, citing Meier repeatedly and nearly always positively. Ancient messenger conventions are the centrepiece for everyone favouring Candidate 2.

The simple problem is that Meier is adamant that these conventions may hold in a host of biblical and extra-biblical messenger contexts *but they do not apply to the Angel of the Lord.*

One factor concerns whether a messenger would announce from whom his message came or just launch into its delivery. Meier is resolute that every commissioned messenger always made such an announcement. Thus, when the Angel of the Lord never makes such a statement, he is not behaving like an ancient messenger. López insists that 'many' ancient examples exist where a message is delivered without introduction.[16]

It's virtually impossible for either scholar to prove his point. Meier asserts that an introduction is always present, a pretty comprehensive claim. López works from the opposite angle, having to confirm that every silence is a real silence: that the messengers never offered any introduction, rather than that their narrators opted not to record a mundane element (supposedly widely understood) that was indeed uttered. Methodologically, Meier's is the slightly easier claim to validate. Even if López is correct about other ancient messengers, he offers no explanation as to why the biblical narrators persistently record no introduction on the lips of the Angel. (There's a chance that an introductory statement occurs in Genesis

---

16. Meier, 'Angel I', p. 49 (cited shortly); 'Angel of Yahweh', p. 58; López, 'Identifying', pp. 6–7.

22:16, but it's neither a guaranteed formula nor a text that either scholar explores.)

Meier explores other ways that the unique Angel of the Lord does not conform to ancient messenger conventions. Angelic messengers communicate between various gods, not between gods and humans; 'when a major god wishes to communicate with a human, he or she can be expected to make a personal appearance'. Meier's support for messenger conventions thus does not extend to support for Candidate 2. His opening and closing comments on the canonical Angel warn *against* relying on ancient conventions:

> However, most of the appearances in the Bible of the phrase *mal'ak YHWH* are not easily explicable by recourse to Near Eastern paradigms . . . The behaviour of the *mal'ak YHWH* in many of these disputed passages is precisely that of a deity and not a deity's messenger.[17]

The problem of missing evidence

The temptation to rely both upon ancient paradigms and Scripture's silences highlights a further difficulty. The very definitions that support Candidate 2 effectively undermine that position. It's an odd argument that sets itself up to fail!

Candidate 2 is defended on the grounds that a messenger can substitute seamlessly for his sender. *We're told that there ought not to be any way to tell the two apart.* Both the messenger and his audience should behave as if the authoritative sender were present.

How, then, do we determine if we're witnessing a messenger rather than his authoritative sender? When dealing with written accounts, as with the Old Testament, we're reliant on the narrator to clarify matters. Yet the Angel of the Lord is hardly presented with any such clarity. He does not introduce himself as does a familiar New Testament messenger: 'I am Gabriel. I stand in the presence of God, and I have been sent to speak to you and to tell you this good news' (Luke 1:19). Any mention the Old Testament Angel makes about God in third-person language is inconclusive. The only

---

17. Meier, 'Angel of Yahweh', pp. 53 (whence also earlier quote), 58.

hint we're given is that this individual bears in his title (*mal'ak yhwh*) the word elsewhere used for a messenger (*mal'āk*).

It's problems like this that Meier highlights. Negatively, the Angel fails to distinguish himself from his sender, as other messengers would be expected to (cf. Gabriel). Positively, the descriptions of the Angel are similar not to descriptions of other messengers but to descriptions of gods and God:

> The only contexts in biblical and ancient Near Eastern literature where no distinction seems to be made between sender and messenger occur in the case of the 'angel (literally 'messenger') of Yahweh' (*mal'ak YHWH*). It is precisely the lack of differentiation that occurs with this figure, *and this figure alone among messengers*, that raises the question as to whether this is even a messenger of God at all . . . It must be underscored that the angel of YHWH in these perplexing biblical narratives *does not behave like any other messenger known in the divine or human realm*. Although the term 'messenger' is present, the narrative itself *omits the indispensable features of messenger activity* and *presents instead the activities which one associates with Yahweh or the other gods* of the ancient Near East.[18]

Alternative evidence from parallel accounts

If an event's narrator does not make clear that we're encountering a messenger, and if the ancient convention is supposed to be that a messenger and his master are functionally interchangeable, it's almost impossible to distinguish the two confidently. López introduces one other potential basis for separating the Angel and God. But yet again his argument steers us towards Candidate 1 rather than Candidate 2.

We're all familiar with the benefits of having several reports of a single event. Sporting telecasts dazzle us with slow-motion replays from multiple angles. Newsworthy events can be pieced together from various media channels. Court cases attempt to establish the truth from the testimony of numerous witnesses. Christian readers are spoiled by having four different Gospel accounts of the earthly ministry of Jesus (though I worry we're too hasty in mashing them

---

18. Meier, 'Angel I', p. 49 (my italics).

together to ask 'What did Jesus do?' rather than first considering 'What did this individual Gospel author want us to understand?'). When we have several reports and a desire to reconstruct the single event they narrate, we can achieve this by comparing and contrasting them.

López wants us to appreciate just how prevalent messengers were, so that we can understand why many narrators do not take the space to furnish the distinguishing detail we might desire. He helpfully contrasts Matthew 8:5–9 with Luke 7:3–8. In the former, a centurion comes to Jesus begging healing for a servant. In the latter account, the centurion conveys his messages via Jewish elders and friends. The elders talk about the centurion, but the friends speak directly to Jesus as if they were the centurion. The point López makes is that messengers speaking on behalf of others were such a familiar concept in the ancient world that Matthew does not need to narrate them at all. Matthew simply presents the story as if the centurion himself had made the trek and entreated Jesus. It's a powerful illustration.

Unfortunately, the illustration probably works against the point López hopes to establish. It undermines his argument in two ways.

First, López successfully illustrates that a single account is insufficient to inform readers about the presence or absence of messengers. If we had only Matthew's report, we would automatically and understandably presume that the centurion himself came and dialogued with Jesus. That is precisely how Matthew presents things. Any messengers are completely transparent. It's only because Luke also reports this event that we have any clue that the centurion himself was not present.

We then realize that most of the Angel passages are isolated, stand-alone reports. We have only single accounts of the Angel's speaking with Hagar, with Abraham on several separate occasions, with Balaam, with Gideon, with Samson's parents and with others. If the Angel is not identified further in those individual accounts, the messenger convention insists that we have no other way of verifying who was present. We have the title 'Angel of the Lord', but we have seen that this is insufficient to prove a separate messenger.

A second undermining occurs when we consider the few events that do have parallel accounts. We've already rehearsed these (at the end of Challenge 1: Gen. 32:22–32 ≈ 48:15–16 ≈ Hos. 12:3–5; 1 Chr. 21:11–17 ≈ 2 Chr. 3:1). The titles 'Angel' and 'God' vary, but there's no other clarification of a distinct messenger's functioning on behalf of God as there is in the centurion example. If we're reliant on parallel accounts for further identification, any that exist typically *conflate* rather than individuate the identities involved.

The standards invoked by López himself, supposedly in favour of Candidate 2, actually serve to promote further the evidence for Candidate 1.

A pause for breath

It seems that the arguments in favour of Candidate 2 are not nearly as convincing as I once hoped they would prove to be.

It's important to admit the attraction of Candidate 2. If God has a special messenger (or a whole fleet of them) and if a commissioned messenger can sound and act just like his sender, the Angel passages become easier to comprehend. Nor would we feel pressed into accepting Candidate 3 and the probability of christophanies, which is usually the alternative option presented.

But the arguments for Candidate 2 prove unpersuasive. The pivotal tenet that supposedly makes the case also undoes it. The expectation that messenger and sender are interchangeable suggests that we later readers of abbreviated reports ought not to be able to distinguish who is present! Without further information we cannot validate a separate messenger. There is little such further information concerning the Angel of the Lord, and what additions we can glean tend to lean towards God (Candidate 1) rather than a commissioned agent (Candidate 2).

Christophany proponents (Candidate 3) will welcome the uncertainty of the messenger solution. They will face their own scrutiny in the next chapter. But we contemplate first a final example that confirms the difficulty of distinguishing the Angel from God and brings together the various factors we've been considering.

A final example

There is merit in working through many Angel passages with the different candidates in mind.

Some are difficult regardless of which candidate we favour. The accounts of the Angel appearing to Gideon (Judg. 6) and to Samson's parents (Judg. 13) can be read with either Candidate 1 or Candidate 2 in view. It seems to me that Candidate 1 works slightly better. In both accounts, those whom the Angel visits do not seem to be aware of any ancient messenger conventions. Gideon panics when he realizes that he has been entertaining the Angel, perhaps a little brazenly, and he expects to die (6:22–23). So too with Samson's parents (13:21–22). The latter account is especially important because Manoah fails to articulate any awareness of messenger conventions: he sees no difference whatsoever between meeting the 'Angel of the Lord' and seeing 'God'.

Still, a strict application of God's agent standing in for God may explain this and passably work for both passages. And, even though a messenger might be expected to introduce himself and to be recognized as an envoy, both passages are odd in that the visiting Angel – whether God or his delegate – withholds his identity until the end of the scene.

One example, though, clearly demonstrates the perils of Candidate 2 and its supposed messenger solution. Let's consider Zechariah 3.

The fourth of Zechariah's eight visions depicts the high priest Joshua on trial. The Angel of the Lord is presiding while an accuser (which is what 'Satan' means) leads the prosecution.

Yahweh himself then speaks: 'The LORD said to Satan, "The LORD rebuke you, Satan! The LORD, who has chosen Jerusalem, rebuke you!"' (3:2). How many participants are involved? Does the Angel introduced in the opening verse speak? Or is the speaking Lord/Yahweh distinct from the Angel, introducing an additional, fourth figure? Either solution strengthens the Candidate 1 case and weakens support for Candidate 2.

Things are simple enough if the Angel and Yahweh are completely identical (Candidate 1). The narrator alternates between two different descriptions ('Angel' and 'Yahweh') and Yahweh speaks about himself in the third person (not uncommon for God and entirely permissible).

Confusion multiplies if the Angel and Yahweh are two distinct figures (Candidate 2). If the 'Yahweh' who speaks at the start of 3:2 is not causing airwaves to move, but rather originating words that are conveyed via his Angel, we again find the two titles collapsing together. We may never be able to distinguish which figure is speaking elsewhere. Nor can we tell whether the Angel's mentions of 'Yahweh' in the third person are verbatim from Yahweh (i.e. third-person self-references at God's dictation) or whether the Angel is paraphrasing a message that was originally worded differently. Or it could be Yahweh himself uttering this speech, distinct from the bystanding Angel, again ratifying third-person self-references. It seems that one or more of three core bases of the Candidate 2 case are jeopardized: (1) Once again, it's almost certain that someone speaks about himself in the third person. A popular argument for distinguishing the Angel and God is neutralized. (2) The labels 'Angel' and 'Lord' are quite likely to be interchangeable in some fashion. The differing labels are the only evidence that prevents us collapsing the two identities together and promoting Candidate 1. (3) Perhaps the Angel rewords the speech he has been given to deliver about Yahweh. If so, we might wonder what paraphrasing was permitted under ancient conventions. We certainly find the Angel failing to speak as if God himself. Which of these will proponents of Candidate 2 willingly sacrifice? Relinquishing any of them damages the credibility of the case usually presented.

And that is just 3:2! Similar confusion proliferates when we brave the remainder of the chapter. The Angel is said to speak (3:3–5) before more clearly bringing a message on behalf of Yahweh (3:6–10). Again, it's a question of which elements of the Candidate 2 case are prioritized and which are relinquished. If labels are definitive, it's odd that 'Yahweh' speaks in 3:2 but 'the Angel' in 3:4 and 3:6. Why is the author inconsistent? Where introductions are informative, and whether or not they're required, why is the speaker or narrator again inconsistent in providing report formulae in 3:7, 3:9 and 3:10, but not in 3:2 or 3:4? If it's persistently the Angel delivering God's words, why does he speak *of* God in the third person in 3:2 but *for* God in the first person elsewhere?

A diagnostic challenge brings all these issues into sharp focus: 'Identify who says "I have taken away your sin" (3:4) and defend your answer.'

Zechariah 3 remains difficult for all interpreters. However, just as an earlier verse (1:12) appears to distinguish between the Angel and Yahweh, so this chapter (and the mention in 12:8) once again draws the two towards interchangeability. Commentators who concede the apparent separation in chapter 1 sound relieved at this return to conflating the two in chapter 3, because it's more consistent with the other evidence in the scene:

> There he was distinguished from YHWH himself (v. 12), but here he is identified with him (v. 2). This appears even more likely inasmuch as Satan is accusing Joshua before the messenger, a notion that finds no support elsewhere in the Bible. The adversary always argues his case before God, not a representative of God, as the very similar scene in the prologue of Job establishes beyond doubt . . . That is, the messenger of YHWH is YHWH as He discloses Himself to human beings.[19]

Summary thoughts

Such accounts leave open the question of *why* God might present himself as the Angel of the Lord. And Scripture certainly never explains *how* God achieves this (or any other tangible manifestation). The common explanation is that this is one of the ways in which God accommodates himself to move among his people safely and undetected. The 'Angel' is God's going-out attire, the cover God adopts to shield his power or his identity. There are many contemporary examples of celebrities disguising themselves so they can experience a normal evening out, of royal figures or bosses veiling their identities so they can move among their underlings and hear honest feedback.

---

19. Eugene H. Merrill, *Haggai, Zechariah, Malachi* (Chicago: Moody, 1994), p. 132. His n. 6 continues to affirm 'the interchangeability of YHWH and Angel of YHWH'.

The Bible repeatedly attests God's desire and commitment to live among humans; this is even the exciting message at the heart of the 'boring' details between Exodus 25 and Numbers 10. The notion of the Angel of the Lord is entirely in keeping with this pattern. God is both willing and able to accommodate himself to forms that can be seen or heard by humans and where any death penalty is suspended. God even opts to appear as mundane and nondescript, as is especially exemplified in the ultimate human-form theophany: the incarnation. It may even be that the Angel is God's biggest hint at this longer-term plan to relate to humans *as* a human. (Even if we resolve in favour of Candidate 2, we add to the dossier of evidence of God's interest in communicating with his world by means they can grasp.)

However, the fact that God accommodates himself as (or through) the Angel of the Lord in the Old Testament and in Jesus of Nazareth in the New Testament does not necessarily equate the Angel and Jesus. We'll consider the difficulties of that equation shortly.

For now, we've seen that the identity of the Angel of the Lord is better understood along the lines of Candidate 1 than Candidate 2. There's plenty of evidence to interpret the Angel *as* God. The suggestion that the Angel is a messenger (or series of messengers) who *represents* God is certainly attractive, but founders on the lack of evidence for ever telling the two of them apart. Once again I have to ask on what grounds scholars such as my colleague Mike Bird suggest that 'it is impossible to absolutely equate them together'.[20] It would seem to me to be wiser not to force the biblical passages to yield a separate, distinct messenger, but to accept only a distinct title under which God forays into his world.

---

20. Michael F. Bird, *Evangelical Theology* (Grand Rapids: Zondervan, 2013), p. 103.

8. CANDIDATE 3: GOD THE SON

We saw earlier that church history has hosted an ongoing duel between those favouring the Angel as a distinct messenger and those interpreting the Angel as a christophany. Candidates 2 and 3 have been pitted against each other for two millennia. Problems with distinguishing a distinct messenger suggest Candidate 2 is an inconclusive option.

Those who prefer Candidate 3 may delight at the difficulties we've found for verifying Candidate 2. The path seems paved for Candidate 3 to race ahead and take the honours. Having shown that the evidence best suggests viewing the Angel of the Lord *as* God rather than as a mundane messenger must surely endorse the long-standing tradition that the divine Son made preincarnate appearances in the Old Testament. We seem to have stronger grounds to expect and discover christophanies.

Yet such a conclusion is far too hasty. Although proponents of Candidates 2 and 3 have been competing for much of two thousand years, the withdrawal of Candidate 2 does not leave Candidate 3 as the sole contender. To return to our metaphor of detectives and courtrooms, Candidate 3 is not the last remaining suspect who must, by process of elimination, be deemed 'guilty'. We've not inadvertently proven the case for christophanies.

This is because interpreters have regularly failed to consider two interrelated factors. The first is that the evidence required to 'convict' Candidate 3 is even more stringent than that for Candidate 2. The second is the possibility of Candidate 1 as a suspect. We need to consider these two factors in more detail. It seems to me that the chances of finding Candidate 3 to best explain the Angel of the Lord are far slimmer than usually allowed.

Factor 1: the difficulties of identifying a separate divine person

As the last chapter detailed, the case for Candidate 2 fails substantially because of the difficulty in distinguishing the Angel from God. Without convincing evidence that the two are distinct, there's no good reason to identify a separate messenger at work. Rather, what evidence we have tends to point towards the Angel as an alter ego of God at work in the world.

The very same factor works against the likelihood of Candidate 3 as well.

Part 2 opened by considering a syllogistic approach:

1. the Angel of the Lord is hard to distinguish from God himself, but
2. the Angel does sometimes seem to be distinct, therefore
3. we need to explain an individual who is simultaneously God and not God.

We've seen plenty of evidence for premise 1, which corresponds to Candidate 1. The Angel and God are all but interchangeable. We've then spent the last chapter realizing just how weak is premise 2; it's all but impossible to distinguish the Angel from God.

However, if premise 2 fails, then the conclusion 3 is equally shaky. Indeed, the evidence for Candidate 3 needs to be even more expertly discerned and argued than the evidence for either of the other two candidates. This is as much a logical corollary as a theological one.

If the Angel of the Lord is to be interpreted as the preincarnate Son, proponents have to master *both* the prior premises. They need to show that the Angel is God. We ourselves have seen this to be fairly straightforward. Because of the historical arm-wrestle concerning Candidates 2 and 3, proponents of Candidate 3 have poured their energy into showing the Angel's divinity. Yet they *also* need to prove that the Angel is distinct from God. This has received far less attention. It has typically been assumed and not investigated. We can see these assumptions in the arguments quoted earlier from Walter Kaiser: like any other angel the Angel of the Lord is supposedly 'sent from' God who, after all, is assumed to be 'invisible'.

Those who would champion Candidate 3 – and Old Testament christophanies – face this hardest challenge. They must simultaneously prove that the Angel is divine *and* that he is distinct from God. This is the most precisely refined identification, so it requires the most rigour in integrating and balancing the elements of both prior candidates. Proponents have to show that the Angel is sufficiently *identified* with God and also *distinguished* from him. Again, the difficulties in distinguishing the Angel in order to promote Candidate 2 are applied to, if not amplified for, those promoting Candidate 3. Yet proponents of Candidate 3 tend to avoid showing that the Angel is distinct from God because to do so would appear to play into the hands of their traditional Candidate 2 opponents.

There is, of course, great irony involved. Supporters of Candidate 2 are happy to allow evidence that the Angel is divine because it illustrates well their case that a distinct messenger can be treated like his sender. Supporters of Candidate 3 are happy to allow evidence that the Angel is divine because they believe he is the preincarnate Son and because they hope evidence of divinity will combat any suggestion that the Angel is a mere creature. Both camps thus pour energy into highlighting the evidence for Candidate 1 and the Angel's divinity while failing to establish the necessary distinction of the Angel from God. Their motives for differentiating the two are dissimilar: one position proposes a distinction between a divine sender and a mundane agent; the other position seeks to differentiate divine persons within the Trinity. Yet both camps uniformly fail to recognize and accomplish the necessity of differentiation, which is largely assumed. Without it, both camps merely further reinforce evidence that favours Candidate 1. (A failure to understand that there are three alternatives rather than two probably explains why a number of scholars can end up muddling their evidence and claims.)

Certainly, those who champion christophanies are guilty of this. They are so fixated on combating the Augustinian alternative that they work hard to *close* the gap between Angel and God – but are not careful enough to ensure that *some* gap remains. Thus Joel Huffstutler's dissertation seeks to be a much needed 'comprehensive biblical theology of the Angel' based on exegesis.[1] He demonstrates the Angel's divinity in detail but merely assumes his numerical distinctiveness because the Angel speaks about God in the third person (discussed last chapter). The same is true with James Borland's seminal book. His first major chapter, which reviewers recognize as 'the heart of Borland's work', is titled 'The Christophany Proved to Be an Appearance of God' and explains that 'the purpose of this chapter is to prove that it was actually *God*, the one, unique Supreme Being of the universe, who appeared to man in the Christophanies'. His first subheading again repeats his emphasis on 'The Proof That God Himself Appeared in the Christophanies'.[2] Although he prejudicially names these appearances of God as 'christophanies', his principal contribution is evidence for the Angel's divinity. Such a methodological flaw afflicts every scholar who campaigns for Candidate 3. A final example comes from Charles Gieschen, where one concerted section begins and ends with a clear but inadequate affirmation of what his section demonstrates:

[T]he second feature of several texts is that both God and the Angel of the Lord are often identified as the same being; they are presented as

---

1. Joel I. Huffstutler, 'He Who Dwelt in the Bush: A Biblical and Historical Theology of the Angel of the Lord' (PhD diss., Bob Jones University, 2007), e.g. pp. 2–3, 16, 58–61, 263.
2. James A. Borland, *Christ in the Old Testament*, 2nd ed. (Fearn: Mentor, 1999), p. 35 (italics original). The review here is of Borland's first edition by William J. Larkin Jr., in *JETS* 23 (1980), p. 162.

indistinguishable . . . Most of the texts that reference the Angel of the Lord depict him as a manifestation of God who is *indistinguishable* from God.

With such a focus on the overlap, Gieschen fails to provide adequate evidence for his final conclusion. Despite the framing and emphasis of his section, we're asked also to accept the Angel as 'a personal being *clearly distinguishable* from God' and 'a *distinct* figure [yet] who functions with divine authority and power'. He offers, only briefly and weakly, his assumptions that Exodus 23:20–21 presents us with an angel who is the Angel of the Lord who is separate from God.[3]

We can certainly appreciate the historical reasons for this focus. Yet they do not make up for the shortcomings in this part of the argument.

Factor 2: the difficulties of identifying which divine person

A similar shortcoming is usually evident when it comes to assuming that the divine identity of the Angel can be narrowed down to be God the Son. Again because of the history of the debate, it seems to most proponents that once they have proven that the Angel is divine their case is complete. As we'll see, some even say this overtly.

Even if we're confident that the Angel of the Lord is both divine and distinct, we've still not demonstrated christophanies. Just because we might determine that the divine Angel is distinct from God, we've not demonstrated that this distinct divine person is the second person of the Trinity. Although I don't think Candidate 3 a likely possibility, there's just as much evidence that the Angel may be God the Spirit. The following scenario showcases how flimsy are some of the grounds used to identify the Son, an approach anticipated centuries ago by Augustine.[4]

---

3. Charles A. Gieschen, *Angelomorphic Christology: Antecedents and Early Evidence*, AGJU 42 (Leiden: Brill, 1998), pp. 57, 67–68 (my italics).

4. E.g. Augustine, *On the Trinity* 2.13. I owe some of the following suggestions to William Graham MacDonald, 'Christology and "The Angel of the Lord"', in Gerald F. Hawthorne (ed.), *Current Issues in*

Even if God the Father is considered invisible, Scripture attests that the Spirit can make bodily appearances; not only does something visible accompany the Spirit's activity at Pentecost (Acts 2:3), but we're told that the Spirit descending on Jesus at his baptism like a dove did so 'in bodily form' (Luke 3:22). Just as the Angel of the Lord is often assumed to be sent by God, so the Old Testament expressly affirms that the Spirit is 'sent' (Ps. 104:30; Isa. 48:16) and otherwise directed by God. There's no doubt that the Spirit is divine and is sometimes described as God's own presence (e.g. Pss 51:11; 139:7). The Spirit speaks in Yahweh's name (e.g. Ezek. 11:5–12) and the whole Bible repeatedly affirms the Spirit's role in communicating for God. The rescue of the Israelites from slavery in Egypt is regularly attributed in Exodus to the 'Angel of the Lord', and later passages identify this rescue and wilderness leading as executed by God's 'Spirit' (Neh. 9:19–21; Isa. 63:9–14; Hag. 2:5). Where the New Testament is allowed to clarify the Old Testament we again find confirmation of the Spirit's being sent, just as angels are, and of his role in communicating God's messages to humanity. Respected commentator F. F. Bruce speaks for many others when he observes in Acts 8 (as in Acts 10) that 'it is difficult to see any real distinction between "the angel of the Lord" and "the Spirit of the Lord"'.[5]

Although these are only brief and imperfect parallels to the arguments used for identifying the Angel as the Son, we find already an impressive and consistent array of evidence that could be used to identify the Angel as the Spirit. Given this array, why is the Son the only triune candidate seriously considered? We must surely baulk when conservative commentator Alec Motyer, attempting to identify the Son, surprisingly asserts that 'There is only one other in the Bible who is both identical with and yet distinct from the Lord.'[6]

Biblical and Patristic Interpretation (Grand Rapids: Eerdmans, 1975), p. 327; Günther H. Juncker, 'Jesus and the Angel of the Lord' (PhD diss., Trinity Evangelical Divinity School, 2001), p. 84, n. 143; and other sources therein.

5. F. F. Bruce, *The Book of the Acts*, NICNT, rev. ed. (Grand Rapids: Eerdmans, 1988), p. 174.

6. J. Alec Motyer, *The Message of Exodus*, BST (Leicester: Inter-Varsity Press, 2005), p. 51.

Further, it seems to me that the Father is never considered as a candidate. It's not my concern to propose him as the exclusive identity of the Angel any more than to prove that the Angel was the Spirit. Yet we've seen that the usual arguments used against the Father – his invisibility, and the supposed impossibility of referring to oneself in the third person or of sending oneself – are substantially weaker than is typically broadcast.

Ultimately, we find that parallels between the Angel of the Lord and the Son of God are based regularly and almost entirely upon circumstantial evidence. This is hardly adequate. Again Kaiser exemplifies the issues. He lists all the grounds for considering that the Angel is divine and marvels at 'this abundance of evidence'. But his only positive proof for narrowing the Angel's identity to 'a preincarnate form of our Lord Jesus Christ' and thus evidence for 'an Old Testament theology of christophanies' is the word 'sent' – a word that does not even occur with the Angel of the Lord. Despite a pious connection with Jesus, this seems a somewhat sandy foundation on which to build any theological edifice.[7]

Put frankly, any concerns to identify the Son in the Old Testament appearances of the Angel of the Lord are driven by external agendas. There's nothing exegetical to cause a search for the Son, and the only textual confirmation is the coincidence that the Son is said to be 'sent' like the Angel is assumed to be. John Walton's excursus starts and ends with pointed complaints:

---

7. Walter C. Kaiser Jr. (with others), *Hard Sayings of the Bible* (Downers Grove: InterVarsity Press, 1996), pp. 191–192; cf. Paul Blackham, 'The Trinity in the Hebrew Scriptures', in Paul Louis Metzger (ed.), *Trinitarian Soundings in Systematic Theology* (Edinburgh: T & T Clark, 2005), pp. 41–42; Ron Rhodes, *Christ Before the Manger* (Grand Rapids: Baker, 1992), pp. 15, 86–87, 91–101 (with some additional functional similarities). Kaiser is probably building his case upon the word 'angel/messenger' being derived from the idea of sending; Blackham clearly asserts the derivation. But biblical scholars are usually alert that a word's historical origins are no guarantee of its contemporary application.

When Justin identified the angel of the Lord as the preincarnate Christ, it was not because of exegetical problems with the Old Testament passages. Rather, it reflected his determined intention to find the triune Godhead in the Old Testament in order to defend the cause of Christianity . . . There is no warrant to move beyond the intention of the author and posit a more theologically sophisticated explanation. The interpretation of the angel as Christ did not arise from exegetical problems but from an aggressive attempt to read distinctives of Christian theology back into the Old Testament with an apologist's agenda.[8]

Both Walton and MacDonald cite and confidently reject the blunt insistence of John Walvoord that 'It is the teaching of Scripture that the Angel of Jehovah is specifically the Second Person of the Trinity.'[9]

Additional factors

In addition to the two major factors that militate against convincing proofs for Candidate 3, there are some other minor impediments. Although Candidate 3 remains logically and theologically plausible, it's simply not exegetically convincing. Sloppy argumentation by proponents further serves to disillusion anyone who seeks solid academic grounds for interpreting the Angel as the preincarnate Son.

We might again single out James Borland, not least because of the impact of his book in establishing the language of 'christophanies' and because, like others, he bases this conclusion almost exclusively upon the Angel of the Lord.

To his credit, Borland includes a section that attempts to clarify 'The Person of the Godhead Who Appeared in the Human-Form Christophanies'.[10] Apart from the fact that using the word

---

8. John H. Walton, *Genesis*, NIVAC (Grand Rapids: Zondervan, 2001), pp. 462, 466.

9. John F. Walvoord, 'The Preincarnate Son of God', *BSac* 104 (1947), p. 166.

10. Borland, *Christ in the Old Testament*, pp. 55–63.

'christophanies' again rather prejudges his conclusion, Borland's investigation is weakened by at least three shortcomings. First, he frightens those who contemplate alternatives by charging them with potential heresy (he names 'Sabellian patripassianism'). This reflects his presupposition that the Angel and God are distinct, even though he hardly proves this. He offers only Zechariah 1:12 as evidence. He intimates that this is one example among many, though we've seen that it's probably the *only* confident example of numerical distinction. The lone example is even less convincing when he has already repeatedly rejected any encounters that occur in visions and when he has allowed that the 'angel of the Lord' in later visions – and he expressly names Zechariah's – may not be the same as the Angel of the Lord he is investigating in the historical narratives.[11]

A second shortcoming is that his section occasionally admits the possibility of physical manifestations being made by both the Father and the Spirit. Indeed, he ultimately offers few reasons against the possibility that these other triune persons may sometimes sporadically share the function of the Angel.

A third shortcoming builds on this and is both significant for our study and detrimental for his. Borland frequently allows that divine invisibility can be relinquished.[12] He may be attempting to counter Augustine's concerns that the *Son* ought to be as invisible as the Father, but Borland succeeds only in showing that *each* member of the Trinity is not constrained to be permanently unseen. This rather deflates his occasional use of John 1:18 to speculate that the Father could not be involved in visible theophanies.

We thus find that Borland is a long way from sufficiently demonstrating that the Angel of the Lord must be identified exclusively as the preincarnate Son. The fact that a leading proponent of Old Testament christophanies has not produced a cogent, coherent, complete argument must lead us to question whether such an argument can be developed and sustained.

It seems to me that similar weaknesses beset any confident assertions of the Angel as the divine Son. We noted above the blunt

---

11. Ibid., e.g. pp. 16–18, 25–26; cf. Rhodes, *Christ Before the Manger*, p. 84.

12. Borland, *Christ in the Old Testament*, pp. 20, 44–45, 86, 96, 99, 103.

claims of Walvoord, arguably Borland's predecessor in championing christophanies. Walvoord triumphantly announces:

> The testimony of Scripture has been so complete on this point that in general scholars who accept the inspiration and infallibility of Scripture have been almost of one voice that the Angel of Jehovah is the Christ of the Old Testament. Not only Christian theologians, but Jewish scholars as well have come to this conclusion.[13]

It may be true that some strands of Jewish scholarship have seen divine tendencies in the Angel, but it's disingenuous to imply that non-Christian Jews have gone so far as to identify the divine Angel as Jesus Christ. Candidates 1 and 3 are being muddled.

Similar intimations and limitations continue to be expressed into the new century. David Murray's valid concern to promote the christological value of the Old Testament rapidly degenerates into an amalgam of captivating rhetoric and plausible theology and incomplete logic that oversteps biblical clarity. Like Borland he moves from allowing that the Father and Spirit sometimes make audible and visible incursions into the world to simplify his methodology and conclusions illogically:

> To prove that this Angel of the Lord was the Son of God, we need only prove the Angel's deity. If the Angel was God, He was the Son of God, for as we have seen above, God was made audible or visible *only* through the Son of God.[14]

---

13. Walvoord, 'Preincarnate Son of God', p. 417. Walvoord praises Borland's book as 'one of the best evangelical presentations of this aspect of Christology to appear this century'; see *BSac* 137 (1980), p. 83.

14. David Murray, *Jesus on Every Page: 10 Simple Ways to Seek and Find Christ in the Old Testament* (Nashville: Thomas Nelson, 2013), pp. 75, 78 (quote on p. 78; my italics). The Angel is the centrepiece of Murray's ninth chapter (pp. 73–85), on 'Christ's Presence: Discovering Jesus in His Old Testament Appearances'.

Summarizing Candidate 3

Although identifying the Angel of the Lord as the Son of God has the longest interpretative history and an encouragingly orthodox tone, it simply cannot be sustained on exegetical grounds.

We must be careful not to commit our own logical fallacies. Just because the arguments for Candidate 3 cannot be sustained does not rule out Candidate 3 entirely. There may be additional theological grounds on which to make this identification. And it may just happen to be true. The point of the present chapter is to show the imprecision of existing exegetical claims. If the Angel is to be identified as the preincarnate Son, a fresh raft of arguments needs to be crafted.

In particular, such arguments need to strike the delicate balance between proving that the Angel is sufficiently like God to be divine and that he is sufficiently distinguished from God to be a distinct person of the Trinity. The former has been well established but the latter has been almost entirely neglected.

Summarizing the Angel

Neglect in distinguishing the Angel of the Lord from God besets not only arguments for Candidate 3 but also those for Candidate 2. When we scratch the surface, there's plenty of evidence to suggest that the Angel is God and not nearly so much to count him as a separate being. We can safely contemplate Candidate 1; we require stronger evidence and arguments to progress further and identify a distinct agent, whether this agent be clarified as some kind of commissioned messenger or the Son of God training for the incarnation.

It's also important to remember how our three candidates connect with Old Testament christophanies. Candidate 1 does not rule out a role for the Son in the work of the Angel; it simply reinforces the lack of evidence for discriminating him as exclusive of the Father and Spirit. Candidate 2 most strongly minimizes any work for the Son (or other members of the Trinity), and there are plenty of advocates and arguments for this interpretation. Only Candidate 3 specifically spotlights the Son. And Candidate 3 requires the most rigorous evidence and argumentation to secure a conviction.

A huge question mark thus hangs over the probability that the Angel of the Lord constitutes specific preincarnate appearances of the divine Son. There simply is not the evidence required in either the Old or New Testaments to substantiate the popular suggestion. Rather, we've seen several lines of argument militating against the likelihood of being able to single out the Son.

We cannot overestimate how significant is the Angel of the Lord to the wider topic of Old Testament christophanies. It would exhaust readers if I were to list the myriad proponents who link the two, but it remains crucial to appreciate that 'This group of [Angel] theophanies is by far the one most widely identified with the Son.'[15] If the Angel is disqualified as the star witness, the case for christophanies all but collapses. It becomes substantially diluted and reminiscent of those pitiable public presentations where the audio-visual display (into which the speaker has invested a disproportionate amount of preparation) fails to work.

To the contrary, as with part 1, we've seen plenty of evidence to suggest that we should marvel at the probable involvement of God the Father. I'm not advocating that the Father works alone. It may be the Father alone or the full undistinguished Trinity operating as the Angel. It may even be that the divine persons take turns in the Angel role. It remains conceivable that the Angel *is* a task regularly assigned to or fulfilled by the Son. Whichever of these is the truest reflection of divine reality, we've seen that there's no convincing exegetical *evidence* for the popular belief that the Angel is a preincarnate appearance of the Son. The limited evidence is entirely circumstantial, nearly unanimously amounting to the functional similarities between the Son whom the Father sends and the Angel of the Lord who – allegedly – is also sent.

The *Five Chinese Brothers* survive because their executioners fail to distinguish between them. Good detective stories keep us in suspense

---

15. Charles A. Gieschen, 'The Real Presence of the Son Before Christ: Revisiting an Old Approach to Old Testament Christology', *CTQ* 68 (2004), p. 116.

because there are several plausible suspects. I reintroduce these illustrations at the close of part 2 to raise three important observations about the enigma that constitutes the Angel of the Lord.

First, it's useful to recognize the attractiveness of an enigma (as we did briefly earlier). Fictional and non-fictional detective stories and investigations remain popular because we're intrigued to watch a mystery being progressively solved. So it's clever marketing when the Angel of the Lord is sold to us akin to the unearthing of the secrets underlying the design and construction of the pyramids. We too can rediscover and reclaim the ancient heritage of early Christianity, a natural thrill of mystery sanctified by the promise of orthodox theology. Juries are selected and instructed to focus on the facts and ignore any media hype; we investigators of the Angel must be alert to any temptation to downplay the facts and embrace the 'obvious' correct conclusion. Scenarios that are plausible and attractive do not necessarily lead to accurate convictions.

Secondly, some authors suggest that individuals in the unfolding drama of the Old Testament *recognized* a distinction between the divine Angel and the God who sent him. That mingles the knowledge we external readers enjoy with the knowledge of the people experiencing the events. The narrator of Judges is clear that what we know about the Angel is different to the perceptions of Manoah and his wife (esp. Judg. 13:16). It's precisely this distinction between us and the participants that makes Disney-like escapades so entertaining: we're let in on the secret of the interchangeable twins or quins, exempt from the confusion experienced by other figures in the story.

Thirdly, the central thesis of part 2 is that a convicting distinction may not be available when it comes to the Angel of the Lord. The two contenders historically, Candidates 2 and 3, fulfil an understandable hope to bring clarity to this enigma. Both are championed from a shared desire to interpret the Scriptures better and to clarify God and his activities in his world. But the understandable preference for closure may remain as unsatisfied on this topic as on many others. Scripture seems no more forthcoming on the identity of the Angel than it is on the date of Jesus' return; despite occasional confident claims throughout church history, there's no clear answer on offer. Our survey inclines towards Candidates 1, 2 and 3 in that order. It also acknowledges that what we can say about Candidate 1 – that the

Angel is 'God' in some fashion – gives the least refinement and is thus, for some if not for many, the least satisfying of the three options. Yet this is where a growing consensus of conservative scholars is willing to leave the matter. We may disdain fictional thrillers that don't lead us to a rewarding finale, but we concede that all too many real-life mysteries remain understood only partially. 'The exact nature or personality of this divine self-revelation are not known precisely because the Scriptures are silent on the question.'[16]

Indeed, the one thing every position agrees is that '*mal'āk*' emphasizes an authorized messenger. We're probably missing the point entirely by dragging the nondescript courier into the spotlight and failing to concentrate on the message he brings or the divine source he represents.

---

16. David M. Howard Jr., *An Introduction to the Old Testament Historical Books* (Chicago: Moody, 1993), pp. 115–116; cf. his *Joshua*, NAC 5 (Nashville: B & H, 1998), p. 160. Others increasingly concur.

PART 3

WHAT DOES THE NEW TESTAMENT CONTRIBUTE?

9. SIGNIFICANT PASSAGES INTRODUCED

Christians have regularly and rightly allowed that the New Testament sometimes clarifies details that Old Testament authors have chosen not to provide. Although Exodus 7 tells us Moses was eighty years old when commissioned by God, we're reliant on Stephen's speech in Acts 7 to learn that Moses had already spent forty years in the wilderness. Exodus earlier praises the work of Moses' mother in hiding him from harm as a baby, but not until Hebrews 11 do we discover that Moses' father also colluded. Moses' opponents in Pharaoh's court are unnamed until 2 Timothy 3:8.

When it comes to contemplating Old Testament christophanies, an important question is whether the New Testament contributes any clarity. We've seen that it's exclusively the New Testament that leads us to consider that God the Father may be invisible, an essential argument in suggesting it's the Son who accomplishes Old Testament appearances. Conversely, the New Testament applies 'angel of the Lord' language to nondescript messengers, not at all assisting the possibility of christophanies. Ironically, if the Angel is to be identified with the Son, it's purely on the basis of New Testament language concerning 'sending'.

So it's appropriate to see if there's any further evidence, positive or negative, that the later testament sheds on the earlier one.

This chapter outlines the major passages pressed into service of christophanies. Chapter 10 then considers the interpretative issues that confront us, so that we can better revisit the New Testament passages in chapter 11. It should be little surprise that I'm not entirely persuaded by the ends to which some of the passages are pressed. At best we find a degree of retrospective clarity that may be claimed from our perspective, even if the Old Testament characters themselves could not have identified and understood the events they experienced. Even our own retrospective clarity should be heavily qualified, though, and we cannot validate exclusive christophanies.

John 8:56, 58

Confronted by stubborn Jews, Jesus declares, 'Your father Abraham rejoiced at the thought of seeing my day; he saw it and was glad.' His opponents are incredulous that a young upstart could have seen the ancient patriarch. But Jesus presses his claim insisting, 'before Abraham was born, I am!'

There are many aspects of the passage over which we could quibble. But the import of the passage is unavoidable: Jesus claims to have existed prior to Abraham's birth. His use of 'I am' is probably an allusion to this special name for God (Exod. 3:13–14). The Jews certainly hear Jesus claiming to be divine because they seek to stone him just as they do 'again' when Jesus later claims to be God (John 10:31–33).

For now, it's important to note that several Old Testament christophanies are supposedly explained by recourse to Jesus' words here. The church father Tertullian speaks for many when he summarizes the importance of John 8: 'it was not the Father that appeared to Abraham but the Son'.[1]

---

1. Tertullian, *Against Praxeas* 22.

John 12:41

John uses similar language when he interprets another Old Testament incident. He says the prophet Isaiah 'saw Jesus' glory and spoke about him'.

John has just cited from Isaiah 53 and Isaiah 6. The latter records the famous theophany where Isaiah 'saw the Lord, high and exalted, seated on a throne; and the train of his robe filled the temple . . . the King, the LORD Almighty' (Isa. 6:1–5).

1 Corinthians 10:4, 9

When the apostle Paul wants to warn the Corinthian Christians against idolatry, he invokes an object lesson from Israel's past. The passage teaches how valuable the Old Testament is for Christian readers. Singling out some major Old Testament occasions of idolatry, Paul explains that 'these things occurred as examples . . . These things happened to them as examples and were written down as warnings for us' (1 Cor. 10:6, 11).

The Israelites had had many benefits and had been saved by God, but many failed to retain God's pleasure. Paul argues that the Corinthians share similar benefits but are in danger of similar idolatry as they eat meat sacrificed in pagan rituals. Food and drink had been one of the Israelites' benefits in the wilderness – and Paul adds that they had drunk 'from the spiritual rock that accompanied them, and that rock was Christ' (10:4).

Paul draws the parallels for his contemporary audience as he urges appropriate behaviour. Among other clear instructions, he implores the Corinthians, 'We should not test Christ, as some of them did' (10:9). This sudden mention of Christ in the Old Testament surprised a number of the scribes who copied 1 Corinthians for later generations; footnotes in English Bibles explain that they sometimes altered this to read, 'We should not test *the Lord* (or *God*)', which is far less startling. We still find 'the Lord' retained in a few versions (including the original NIV), but translators and scholars now almost universally favour that Paul wrote 'Christ' in 10:9. Besides, that is what he wrote in 10:4, which has not been challenged or altered.

Moreover, Paul's warnings do not come from a single event but from several. His mentions of drinking from Christ and testing Christ apply at least throughout the forty-year period that the Israelites wandered in the wilderness, evoking hints and episodes recorded in Exodus 17 and 32 and Numbers 16, 17, 20 and 21 – the start and end of those forty years.

Scholars as well as lay interpreters are thus convinced this is a pivotal passage. One is confident that 'This is the one passage in the NT where everyone admits that we have a clear example of Christ's pre-existent activity in OT history.' Another, over a century ago in a prominent encyclopedia, collated several of the interpretative steps to expound in more detail:

> Not less did the testimony of Paul, I Cor. x. 4, and the practise of the Greek Fathers from Justin Martyr, who identified the 'angel of the Lord' with the Logos, furnish excuse for conceiving also the theophanies of the Old Testament as christophanies.[2]

Jude 5

Bible readers are sometimes disturbed to learn that not every scribe copied the Scriptures flawlessly. The confusion presented by 1 Corinthians 10:9 is even more evident in the fifth verse of the short letter of Jude. (I've deliberately written 'letter *of* Jude' to reinforce an earlier lesson. This means at least the epistle *described as* 'Jude' or even *ascribed to* him, and I have no reason to doubt that the letter was actually *written by* him.)

Scribes have had a difficult time estimating what the verse originally said. Modern scholars are no less perplexed. In passing, Jude describes how God 'at one time delivered his people out of

---

2. Respectively, Anthony Tyrrell Hanson, *Jesus Christ in the Old Testament* (London: SPCK, 1965), p. 10; Emil F. Kautzsch, 'Theophany', in Samuel M. Jackson (ed.), *The New Schaff-Herzog Encyclopedia of Religious Knowledge* (orig. 1911; repr. Grand Rapids: Baker, 1969), vol. 11, p. 403.

Egypt, but later destroyed those who did not believe'. Where I have written 'God', most English Bibles record 'the Lord'. That is not particularly contentious. But the Greek manuscripts attest a whole range of different words and phrases here; many write 'the Lord' or 'God', but some favour 'Jesus' or '(the) Lord Jesus' or even 'God Christ'. A substantial number of scholars argue that one of these latter is more likely to have been Jude's original. Thus the ESV has good grounds for presenting readers with 'Jesus, who saved a people' in the events of the exodus. Many others who think that Jude wrote 'Lord' believe he was referring to the Lord Jesus rather than to the Lord God.

Thus, although there's still some debate over what Jude *wrote* and whom he *meant*, there are good reasons to find here another reference to Jesus' Old Testament activity. 'One must conclude that Jude viewed the Messiah as present (in his preincarnate state) and active throughout the history of the Old Testament.'[3]

Minor claims and assumptions

These four main texts are joined by several other substantiating claims and assumptions presented in the New Testament. Especially when combined with the two passages from John, these can even move towards suggesting not just that Old Testament figures saw the Son but that they recognized something of his personal distinction from God.

John 8 names Abraham, and John 12 claims that Isaiah saw and spoke about Jesus. Hebrews 11:26 seems to certify the same grasp for Moses, who 'regarded disgrace for the sake of Christ as of greater value than the treasures of Egypt'. The apostle Peter implies that every prophet knew something of this, because of 'the Spirit of Christ in them' who 'predicted the sufferings of the Messiah and the glories that would follow' (1 Peter 1:11). Thus these prophets 'made careful searches and inquiries, seeking' to know more

---

3. Robert L. Reymond, *A New Systematic Theology of the Christian Faith*, 2nd ed. (Nashville: Thomas Nelson, 2002), p. 534.

(1:10–11 NASB). And indeed answers were 'revealed to them', that their discoveries applied to a future, New Testament, generation (1:12).

Certainly, many other minor claims are consistent with the idea of the Son's activity in the Old Testament. Some are simple confirmations of his eternal existence 'from the beginning' (e.g. 1 John 1:1; John 1:1). Jesus himself strongly asserts this: 'I am the Alpha and the Omega, the First and the Last, the Beginning and the End' (Rev. 22:13). Other references can be found in Paul, along with Jesus' own discussions of having 'come', as if his incarnation were only a newer movement in his longstanding existence.[4]

There are other hints, though these can be subtle or complex to demonstrate. Suffice to say, the New Testament is both explicit and implicit in teaching the presence and activity of the Son in Old Testament times prior to his incarnation. This is a standard element of Christian doctrine and not in dispute here. The question is whether we can detect any of this activity within the pages of the Old Testament, or whether we can learn about it only after the fact when we turn to the New Testament. More precisely, what might be said about potential christophanies? We pause to consider a major difficulty with our task before returning to consider in more depth the passages outlined here.

---

4. E.g. Mark 1:38; 2:10; 10:45; John 17:5; Rom. 8:3; 2 Cor. 8:9; Gal. 4:4; Phil. 2:6–7; Col. 1:15–18.

10. ISSUES OF WORKING BACKWARDS

N. T. Wright is now a famous biblical scholar. Before his name was widely known, he outlined a terribly sensible observation: our descriptions of the past are heavily influenced by our knowledge and language of the present. He reprised an example already circulating among British evangelicals concerning the way Paul describes Jesus in Colossians 1:15:

> The language Paul uses to refer to him before his human conception and birth is often borrowed from his later human life, just as we say 'the Queen was born in 1926', not meaning that she was then already Queen, but that *the person we now know as Queen* was born that year. Thus 2 Corinthians 8:9, 'For you know the grace of our Lord Jesus Christ, that though he was rich, yet for your sakes he became poor': not that the pre-existent one was already Jesus, the Messiah, but that *the person we now know as Jesus, the Messiah*, is to be identified as God's pre-existent agent.[1]

---

1. N. T. Wright, *The Epistles of Paul to the Colossians and to Philemon*, TNTC 12 (Leicester: Inter-Varsity Press, 1986), p. 69 (italics original).

I myself have attempted to be careful to write more about 'the pre-existent Son' and less about 'Jesus' in the Old Testament. But I've included such references on occasions, perhaps without anyone even noticing.

What is going on?

We do this all the time. It happens especially when there's a change of name or status. That change can sometimes be quite substantial. Queen Elizabeth's father, 'King George VI', spent the first four decades of his life known as 'Prince Albert'. One school teacher loved to quiz us on the capital of Upper Volta – it's Ouagadougou – even though by then the nation had changed its name to Burkina Faso. It seems there are few countries in Africa that have not been through such a name change; keeping one's maps and knowledge and language current is nearly impossible.

Our speech and writing are thus filled with potential anachronisms.

It's perfectly understandable why we tolerate anachronisms. Sometimes we're unaware that a change has occurred or we're otherwise living in the past. More commonly, we choose a contemporary label that is the most convenient shorthand for what we're trying to communicate in the present. Conversation is far more efficient if we use familiar names such as 'Woody Allen' and 'Bill Clinton' than if we more pedantically mention, respectively, 'Allen Stewart Konigsberg' or 'William Blythe III'.

Widespread biblical examples

It should be no surprise that biblical authors do the same thing. Their goal is to communicate with a particular audience, so they choose terms that effect that communication. Sometimes they're alert to this updating; at other times there's no indication whether or not they know about the possible imprecision or anachronism.

Exploring some of the myriad biblical examples gives us a taste for the phenomenon and for how prevalent it is in every part of Scripture.

Common minor examples

Genesis 14 narrates how two coalitions of kings clash; Lot is subsequently captured, and then rescued by Uncle Abraham. Several locations are given. The narrator takes time to draw overt links familiar to later readers: 'This occurred at X, which is now known as Y.' The places he explains tend to be those that recur in Genesis and later Scripture. A third layer of identification can then be added by modern commentators, who explain all this to contemporary readers. Respected commentator Gordon Wenham further updates the map for us: 'Four kings, led by Kedorlaomer of Elam (part of Iran), conquered the Jordan valley [a term unused in Gen. 14] . . . Melchizedek, the priest-king of Salem (probably Jerusalem) . . .'[2]

The same phenomenon occurs in Joshua 15. At least nine conquered cities of Canaan are further identified by additional, contemporary names.

There are several reasons why we know about these name changes. First, on some occasions, such as the ones outlined here, the author is clear that he is providing alternative identifiers. Secondly, it's often only later in the biblical story that we read of a place receiving its name. Familiar locations such as 'Beersheba', 'Bethel', 'Gilgal', 'Dan' and 'the cities of Samaria' are all mentioned in stories before they're formally named. That's no problem for later readers, who are already *now* familiar with those locations. Sometimes the gap can be substantial; Dan offers a good example. The city is mentioned as early as the account of Lot (Gen. 14:14) and is sighted at Moses' death (Deut. 34:1) even though it's not named until near the end of the subsequent conquest of Canaan (Josh. 19:47; Judg. 18:29). Thirdly, a narrator can even explain in detail what is going on. The most overt 'translation' from past to present is offered in 1 Samuel 9. Saul and his servant are about to encounter Samuel and call him a 'seer' (1 Sam. 9:11, 18, 19). To make sense of that terminology, the narrator forewarns his readers that their 'seer' is equivalent to 'today's "prophet"' (9:9 ESV).

---

2. Gordon J. Wenham, 'Genesis', in D. A. Carson et al. (eds.), *New Bible Commentary*, 4th ed. (Leicester: Inter-Varsity Press; Downers Grove: InterVarsity Press, 1994), pp. 71–72.

Elsewhere, Bible authors use formulae such as 'until this day' to acknowledge the passing of time.

It's not just names that can be 'translated' this way. All sorts of other measures and customs are updated for newer generations of readers. The donations solicited by King David for temple building are measured, five centuries later, in contemporary Persian currency (1 Chr. 29:7). The authors of the Gospels and Acts regularly explain titles, rituals and other foreign concerns for their readers.[3]

Sometimes it's as simple as shared knowledge stealing into an author's account. Genesis and Exodus make several mentions of the Philistines, even though that people group probably did not immigrate and become Israel's famous nemesis for another six to ten centuries. The very first chapter of Israel's time in the wilderness lets slip that it will take forty years to reach Canaan (Exod. 16:35), even though it's more than a dozen months and five dozen detailed chapters of Scripture before that delay is actually incurred (Num. 14:33–34). The preceding verses describe how a sample of manna is kept for the benefit of future generations and stored with the ark or tablets of the covenant (Exod. 16:32–34), even though neither ark nor covenant has yet been given. Priests and their consecration are mentioned by God when he formally constitutes the nation of Israel (Exod. 19:22–24), even though neither of these is yet detailed (Exod. 28 – 29; Lev. 1 – 7) or instituted (Lev. 8 – 9).

Major examples

There are two substantial examples that warrant a little more attention. These confirm just how prevalent is the practice of using new labels for old situations.

Exodus 6:3 is controversial in biblical studies. God tells Moses, 'I appeared to Abraham, to Isaac and to Jacob as God Almighty, but by my name the LORD [Yahweh] I did not make myself known to them.' This is consistent with the fact that God's special name is

---

3. Primary examples are Matt. 1:23; 27:33, 46; Mark 3:17; 5:41; 7:3–4, 11, 34; 12:42; 15:16, 22, 34, 42; John 1:38, 41–42; 4:9; 9:7; 12:3; 20:16; Acts 4:36; 9:36; 13:8; 23:8. The concentration in Mark and John teaches us something about their intended readership.

usually thought to originate when he first appeared to Moses a few chapters previously (3:14–15). But what then are we to make of the 165 occurrences of 'Yahweh' in Genesis (and another three earlier in Exodus)?

Scholars are evenly divided. Perhaps slightly more than half accept the verse as it stands (esp. HCSB, NLT, CEV). This means that the story of Genesis has been written using language known to later readers but unknown to the actual individuals in the story. Others baulk at this possibility, but their solution is not very different. They insist that the patriarchs knew and used the name 'Yahweh', but concede there was still lots left to learn about the God whom this describes. That's the sense inherent in the international edition of the revised NIV: 'I did not make myself *fully* known to them.' Either way, it's obvious that what later readers (including ourselves) comprehend about Yahweh in Genesis is more than Abraham, Isaac and Jacob knew.

The second major example is surprising in a different way. Even the youngest Sunday school student knows that God changed Abram's name to Abraham (Gen. 17:5). Yet we almost universally use the longer version, even though he bore it less than half his life. I have used it several times for incidents where he was still known as Abram. This convention is followed even in Scripture. Exodus 6:3 talks about God's appearances to 'Abraham' (cf. Lev. 26:42; Josh. 24:2–3), though many occurred before Genesis 17. None of the Gospels uses the shorter name. Stephen, Paul, Hebrews and James refer to Abram prior to his name change expressly using the longer, anachronistic 'Abraham' (Acts 7:2–8; Rom. 4; Gal. 3; Heb. 7:1–10; 11:8–10; Jas 2:23). Because John 8:58 is almost certainly a reference to Abram's birth (so NIV, NASB) even Jesus follows this practice. Some christophany proponents also overtly recognize and follow the convention.[4]

What is regularly overlooked is that the authors of the New Testament (and other Christian works) are so comfortable with this convention that they even revise the *text* of the Old Testament!

---

4. E.g. Jonathan Stephen, *Theophany: Close Encounters with the Son of God* (Epsom: Day One, 1998), p. 44, nn. 1, 3.

Genesis 15:6 is famous as a model of faith. The Hebrew text does not name Abram at this point but simply affirms '*he* believed the LORD'. The Septuagint (the Greek translation of the Old Testament) does what modern Bible translators sometimes do and clarifies '*Abram* believed God' (cf. NIV, HCSB). It's the Septuagint that scholars uniformly accept as the source of the quote in the New Testament. Yet when Paul and James use the line (Rom. 4:3; Gal. 3:6; Jas 2:23) they update the text of the Old Testament to read '*Abraham* believed God.' (We know it's the Septuagint that Paul and James are citing because of the shift from 'LORD' to 'God'. That is another revision Christian readers accept without really noticing. It's certainly not a theological dilemma unless one holds an extremely rigid view of translation.)

These two major examples are extremely important. At the very least they demonstrate the common-sense convention we're considering in this chapter: authors use contemporary language that communicates meaningfully in *their* day. In turn, we have to be wary of retrojecting such later words and concepts into earlier contexts. Certainly, with the example of Abraham, we must acknowledge that Stephen, Paul, Hebrews, James and Jesus use a name for Abram that would have been irrelevant in the original contexts they describe. The same is true for the name or meaning of 'Yahweh' throughout Genesis.

The significance of these examples

For many people the word 'anachronistic' conveys a pejorative tone. Something anachronistic is a mistake. Pedants scrutinize movies and complain when something is inappropriate, such as Christian imagery used in pre-Christian settings or firearms employed before the invention of gunpowder. On its own an 'anachronism' simply refers to something 'out of time' in some way. And, for many endeavours, being out of time can indeed be a mistake.[5]

The kinds of biblical examples we're concerned with include anachronisms in only a limited sense – and only if they are misused.

---

5. See for examples, P. J. N. Lawrence, '"Oh No, He's Still Wearing His Watch!": Avoiding Anachronism in Old Testament Translation', *BT* 59 (2008), pp. 14–17.

It's entirely reasonable to claim that 'the Queen was born in 1926', unless we mistakenly imply or infer she was Queen at that time. People regularly recount the past in terms that make sense in the present.

All this can become a surprisingly tricky prospect. It makes us contemplate exactly how Scripture works, especially when many of its constituent elements describe earlier eras for contemporary audiences. It's further complicated when Christians profess there's also ongoing value for today. Consider John's Gospel. It narrates events of Jesus' earthly ministry around AD 30; it was written for readers in another location and speaking another language later that century; Christians believe God uses the same document to speak to subsequent generations of readers in many languages. The Old Testament documents span even longer time frames, some of which are difficult to pin down with any precision. When we come to produce the (fictitious) New Revised International Standard Version, which language conventions should we follow? To pick just one example: How do we convey the Israelites' contributions to David's collection for the temple in 1 Chronicles 29:7? Do we use terms appropriate for David's day? Do we honour the descriptions given by Chronicles more than five centuries after David? Do we use contemporary figures that communicate to modern readers? (Do we express the quantities of precious metals by currency or by weight? And do we use dollars or pounds or euros; grams or ounces?)

Few of us are called to be Bible translators. But we're all called to be Bible readers. What do we expect when we read? Sometimes it's obvious that we're spanning such distances, reading in English about a concept recorded by John in Greek concerning the Aramaic original of Jesus' day. But it's often not quite so straightforward. What is a 'penny' worth? The word occurs in every major and minor translation I've checked, but it means different things in different versions. In the fourteenth century, just as the first English translations were starting to flourish, a penny was a day's wages. That is thus what 'penny' means in the AV/KJV translations of Matthew 20. Of course, that is no longer a helpful comparison, and the newest versions devalue the word to denote trivial sums (e.g. Matt. 5:26; 10:29).

How do we know if what we're reading refers to our day, to the era of the author, or to the time of the events being narrated?

Ultimately, we require additional knowledge to suspect or detect that an anachronism has occurred. We saw in chapter 7 that we need parallel accounts to know whether an authority speaks for himself or through delegated messengers. For anachronisms we need some other literary or archaeological information to cause and confirm suspicion that something is out of place. Without such confirmation, the safest 'sphere' for interpretation is the one in which the biblical words were written. We're on less certain ground if we try to estimate what was taking place prior to that time.

So I do not want the word 'anachronism' to be taken pejoratively. Neither am I suggesting that any attempts to read the Bible are hopeless! Scripture remains the core of God's revelation. Yet there are places where we have to concede that God has not revealed every fact with equal clarity. Genesis 16 does not actually pronounce judgment one way or the other upon Abraham's attempt to foster an heir through Hagar. Daniel 1 simply cannot be milked for dietary advice. (It's almost certainly not about nutrition. If anything, it's a call to avoid conforming to the latest fad.) Though two Gospels mention Satan's involvement, we're left to speculate what human motivations spurred Judas to betray Jesus. Both Old and New Testaments are clear that Scripture is discriminating in what it presents. We see this in the careful selectivity and structuring of some historical accounts (e.g. Judges; Acts) and in overt statements (e.g. Deut. 29:29; John 20:30; 21:25).

We simply need to be alert to the ways that writers report history. The possibility of biased reporting can of course be abused; the history of biblical interpretation is littered with readers massaging the text to match their own presuppositions. But ignoring the contexts and agendas of the biblical authors is poor interpretation too. We can summarize the issues presented in this chapter by looking at two final examples, one from each testament.

We've already noted some of the ways Genesis may update its story for a later generation. Wenham rehearses some of the examples and their implications:

> Particularly names of places and peoples seem to have been modernized in Genesis, e.g. Dan (14:14), Ur of the *Chaldeans* (15:7), possibly

Philistines (21:32, 34), and Arameans (31:20, 24). These terms may be, strictly speaking, anachronisms, but they represent the narrator's way of clarifying the story for his contemporary readers, just as a modern writer might describe Babylon as being near Baghdad, although Baghdad did not exist in Nebuchadrezzar's day. Thus, when we read the story of Joseph, we view his career from the standpoint of a later writer, who has described Joseph in terms that made sense to the first readers rather than with the terminology that a contemporary of Joseph would have used.[6]

The same observations can be made for the way Luke recounts (some of) the history of the early church in Acts. He occasionally uses words such as 'elders' that may reflect the later date at which he writes rather than the terms used when Paul founded these congregations (Acts 14:23; 20:17):

> Since there is no mention of elders in the letters of Paul prior to the
> Pastoral Epistles [towards the end of Paul's life], it is often argued that
> the reference here is an anachronism . . . The most, however, that we
> may deduce from these facts is that Luke has used a term current in
> his own time to refer to leaders who may possibly have been known
> by other designations in the earlier period.[7]

What is at stake?

As we move towards our key New Testament passages, we should ponder the interpretative lessons learned from this chapter. In short, we should be cautious when using a later author's language to reconstruct too precisely the history being narrated.

---

6. Gordon J. Wenham, *Genesis 16–50*, WBC 2 (Waco: Word, 1994), pp. xxvi–xxvii (italics original); cf. Michael A. Grisanti, 'Inspiration, Inerrancy, and the OT Canon: The Place of Textual Updating in an Inerrant View of Scripture', *JETS* 44 (2001), esp. pp. 582–588.
7. I. Howard Marshall, *The Acts of the Apostles*, TNTC 5 (Leicester: Inter-Varsity Press, 1980), p. 241.

We considered earlier the message of Exodus 6:3. The characters discussing 'Yahweh' in Genesis may not have used this exact name for God. Even if they did use the name, they had not experienced as much of his faithful saving identity as would the exodus generation. Conservative commentators are thus mostly circumspect about reconstructing what the patriarchs would have said or known about 'Yahweh'.

We should be equally circumspect about what we ascribe to people whose words and thoughts are recorded at later times for later readers. We should be alert to the possibility of appropriate biblical anachronisms. We can heartily agree that Abraham camped at a place that came to be known as Bethel (Gen. 12:8; 13:3) but we must not automatically assume that this is what he himself called that location (or what he called himself at the time!).

Again, some of us can be unnerved by this apparent separation between historical events and their narration. I am keen not to induce unnecessary angst, and I am not using these observations to deny the historicity of biblical events. At the same time, we read the Bible responsibly when we remember that we're dealing with later summaries for later audiences. Thoughtful interpreters show that this is a legitimate view of Scripture:

> *anachronism:* a detail or word in a story that does not fit the time period
> of the story. Often anachronisms can be understood as clarifications
> or adjustments made to the text at a later time.[8]

> The reference to the *cities of Samaria* [in 1 Kgs 13:31–32] is
> anachronistic in terms of the time and setting of the story (not until
> Ahab's reign, when he built Samaria, did the north acquire the name,
> Samaria), but it was not anachronistic to the time of writing . . . [The
> *darics* of 1 Chr. 29:7] were Persian gold coins, possibly named for
> Darius I (520–486 B.C.), and therefore anachronistic to David's era,
> but not necessarily to the time of writing by the Chronicler. He used

---

8. John H. Walton, Victor H. Matthews and Mark W. Chavalas, *The IVP Bible Background Commentary: Old Testament* (Downers Grove: InterVarsity Press, 2000), p. 812.

the daric, the current unit of exchange, to evaluate the offering of
Israel's leaders.[9]

The possibility of appropriate anachronisms applies especially to
speeches recorded in Scripture. Again, I seek neither to deny that
these speeches occurred nor to allow that they have been substantially
altered. Yet we know they have undergone *some* transformation before
reaching us. We know that various Old Testament speeches occurred
in various languages (e.g. Gen. 42:23; 2 Kgs 18:26 = Isa. 36:11; Ezra
4:7; Dan. 1:4). Examples from the Gospels in footnote 3 of this
chapter explain, as part of the text of Scripture, that words spoken
by Jesus and his disciples were delivered in Aramaic even though we
have only the Greek record of them. Few of us even read them in
Greek; we're content that our English Bibles are an adequate
third-generation representation of the original Aramaic discourses.
So, too, with Paul's speeches in Acts. At least twice Luke reveals that
the speeches he has recorded in Greek were uttered in Hebrew
or Aramaic (Acts 20:40 = 22:2; 26:14). Indeed, all the speeches in
Acts have been subject to scholarly scrutiny. While it's sometimes
fashionable to dismiss them as Luke's literary fictions, we can accept
them as historically reliable. Yet we must simultaneously accept that
'historically reliable' means we have an adequate *summary* of what
was said and not a record that is exhaustive or verbatim. Luke himself
confirms he did not record everything (e.g. 2:40; 14:1–3).[10]

Put simply, what we read may not be the exact words or even the
precise sentiment conveyed on the original occasion. A final example
alerts us to both issues.

The centurion supervising Jesus' crucifixion famously confesses,
'Surely this man was the Son of God!' (Mark 15:39). First, we may

---

9. Harvey D. Hartman, 'I–II Kings' and 'I–II Chronicles', in Edward
   E. Hindson and Woodrow Michael Kroll (eds.), *The KJV Bible
   Commentary* (Nashville: Thomas Nelson, 1994), pp. 674, 798
   (emphases original).

10. E.g. John R. W. Stott, *The Message of Acts*, BST (Leicester: Inter-Varsity
    Press, 1990), pp. 69–72; Ben Witherington III, *The Acts of the Apostles*
    (Grand Rapids: Eerdmans, 1998), pp. 39–49, 116–120.

reasonably suggest these were not the only words he said that day. We know others were passing comments that were not recorded (e.g. 15:29–32). Mark seems to have recorded this sentence for a particular purpose. Given that Luke 23:47 records a different sentence, it's unclear whether one is a reinterpretation of the other or whether the centurion uttered both. Secondly, while it would be a stunning on-the-spot conversion at the crux of salvation history, there's no reason to think the centurion was among the first humans to ascertain and articulate a doctrine of the Trinity. To a Roman the phrase 'Son of God' was used for acclaiming the emperor. It's the Roman equivalent of the Jews' (supposedly) sarcastic exaltation of Jesus as 'Messiah . . . king of Israel' a few verses earlier (15:32). But it suits Mark's purpose perfectly to record this theological double entendre; his whole Gospel is focused on following Jesus as 'Son of God' (1:1). 'Whatever the centurion might credibly have meant in a merely historical reading, in the light of the rest of the Gospel his words tell the readers far more.'[11] Mark's use of the phrase is not automatically correlated with the centurion's own understanding.

(The same applies to the rescue of Shadrach, Meshach and Abednego from the fiery furnace. The incredulous king spots a fourth man in the fire, whom he describes as 'a son of the gods' and God's sent 'angel' [Dan. 3:25, 28]. In keeping with tradition and the KJV/NKJV translation – 'like the Son of God' – this is still sometimes considered a christophany.[12] But most scholars are circumspect about the different nuances the phrase would hold for polytheistic Nebuchadnezzar, for later Jewish readers and, only eventually and derivatively, for trinitarian Christians.[13])

---

11. Richard J. Bauckham, *Jesus and the God of Israel* (Milton Keynes: Paternoster, 2008), p. 266.

12. E.g. Ron Rhodes, *Christ Before the Manger* (Grand Rapids: Baker, 1992), pp. 97–98; Stephen R. Miller, *Daniel*, NAC 18 (Nashville: B & H, 1994), pp. 123–124; Dale Ralph Davis, *The Message of Daniel*, BST (Nottingham: Inter-Varsity Press, 2013), pp. 57–58.

13. E.g. Sidney Greidanus, *Preaching Christ from Daniel* (Grand Rapids: Eerdmans, 2012), pp. 94–98.

So we approach with humility the coming chapter and its survey of New Testament passages. The apostle Paul concedes he does not yet know everything (1 Cor. 13:12). We'd be wise to emulate him.

The New Testament readily attests that God the Son has always been active throughout human history (and even before). But it does not provide the clarity it's sometimes reputed to. It certainly does not clarify any particular Old Testament christophanies and invite us to turn to specific verses and discover there the preincarnate Jesus. Let's consider the passages one by one, following the same order introduced in chapter 9 above.

John 8:56, 58

For a start, it's helpful to notice that John 8:58 is not directly relevant. It's certainly momentous that Jesus can say 'I am' just as Yahweh does in the Old Testament. But that does not tell us anything more than that Jesus identifies with God. If it bears any relevance to christophanies, it allows that the Son may have participated in appearances of God but it does not in any way single out those theophanies as his domain exclusively.

It's 8:56 that seems to peg Jesus hanging around in Abraham's time in some tangible fashion. Yet there are many things about this verse that are inconclusive. 'Jesus' statement about Abraham here, though most remarkable, is not entirely clear.'[1]

Foremost, the verse does not actually claim anything about theophanies! Abraham was excited that he might see Jesus' 'day' – and there's no further clarity concerning what this means. We've discovered that verbs of seeing in John can, as in English, refer as much to comprehension and believing as to physical eyesight. Even if the verse means that Abraham looked forward to a day when Jesus would physically appear in theophanies, it seems an odd way to describe this.

In turn this alerts us to the fact that there are no concrete occasions to which Jesus appears to be alluding. Certainly, there are several occasions when God 'appeared' to Abraham (e.g. Gen. 12:7; 17:1; 18:1). There may be other allusions to God's direct action that may involve visible appearances (15:17–20; 18:22–33; 24:7). The most popular is where 'the word of the LORD came to him' (15:4); proponents argue this sense of 'word' should be understood in the light of John 1 and the way Jesus is there described as the 'Word' that eventually became flesh. But none of these refers to Abraham's rejoicing. If Jesus is overtly teaching about christophanies, he is making a claim that applies somehow to Abraham's life but one we cannot further verify or explore from the pages of the Old Testament.

If there's to be an Old Testament connection, it's with the occasions when Abraham and Sarah delighted at the birth of Isaac in their old age (17:17–22; 21:1–7). Abraham obviously didn't think his infant son was the actual arrival of Jesus. Rather, Isaac was the primary proof that all God's promises were indeed coming to fruition. Abraham saw and rejoiced that God's plans were in motion.

There are other ways to understand Abraham's 'seeing' Jesus' day. It probably suggests Abraham had some degree of prophetic foresight and rejoiced in what he saw of God's rescue starting to occur. It's also possible that Jesus is referring to Abraham's still being alive in the first century: Abraham is in paradise rejoicing that Jesus'

---

1. Herman N. Ridderbos, *The Gospel According to John*, tr. John Vriend (Grand Rapids: Eerdmans, 1997), p. 320.

day has finally arrived. Though this is the least popular option, it is consistent with the debate Jesus has just been having about whether Old Testament figures died or not (John 8:51–53) and is given some credence by scholars of John's Gospel. Where Christian theology is allowed to influence biblical interpretation, John 8:56 is as much consistent with a theology of Abraham's 'post-existence' as with Jesus' pre-existence.

Even if we insist that the verse describes Abraham's seeing Jesus in Abraham's own era, we must be careful about presuming what Abraham himself understood. *Jesus* describes Abraham's experience as 'my day', but this tells us nothing of what Abraham could have articulated. We're told that Manoah met someone *we* know as the Angel of the Lord while his own insights remained stunted (Judg. 13:16). Without any Old Testament verification, we can claim nothing more than that Jesus later describes Abraham's insights as applying, somehow, to Jesus.

It is thus going much too far to claim that Abraham both met Jesus and comprehended his identity. We cannot follow Anthony Hanson's insistent conclusion:

> John 8.56 contains not only the claim that Abraham was told all about the future incarnation, but also the claim that he actually saw Christ. The language is no doubt intentionally ambiguous, but we must understand that Abraham saw Christ, and was justified, like all Christians, through faith in Christ.[2]

If nothing else, Hanson exemplifies that the wording used at a later date may not accurately reflect the era being described. Drawing on Genesis 15:4 before Abram's name change, Hanson is content that the longer 'Abraham' communicates adequately to his twentieth-century readers. Nor does Hanson explain why such an important and allegedly common doctrine was cast in intentionally ambiguous language.

---

2. Anthony Tyrrell Hanson, *Jesus Christ in the Old Testament* (London: SPCK, 1965), p. 125; cf. Jonathan Stephen, *Theophany: Close Encounters with the Son of God* (Epsom: Day One, 1998), p. 51.

It seems to me that the most trinitarian mileage we can gain from John 8 is that Jesus is *adding* himself to Old Testament expectations of God and God's activities. Jesus claims to be part of the future that Abraham anticipated. We cannot determine anything of what Abraham himself actually comprehended. And, if this describes any way in which Abraham sighted God in a visual sense, it claims nothing more than that Jesus was active *with* God the Father; it contributes nothing to the quest for Jesus' exclusive participation in Old Testament theophanies.

This point seems largely conceded by those who endorse christophanies. Although some such as Hanson construct part of their edifice on the foundation of John 8:56, most ignore the verse altogether. Among those surveyed, it is otherwise really addressed only by Walter Kaiser, who concludes as I have that Abraham foresaw and rejoiced at whatever inklings God gave him of God's future plans. Kaiser himself warns that we cannot identify the details or language Abraham might have articulated.[3]

John 12:41

This same caution should be applied to the other passage from John, which is more regularly invoked. Here it's John (rather than Jesus) who clarifies that a past theophany can be said to include the Son as well. It requires additional doctrinal assumptions beyond this passage to assert that John is claiming an exclusive christophany.

As a whole, John's Gospel is heavily concerned with the Son's glory and especially the process of the Father's glorifying him. The Gospel is written to discuss various responses of belief and unbelief in the signs performed by Jesus, hoping to encourage faith (John 20:30–31). These themes of glory and (un)belief are prevalent in the passage under scrutiny (12:37–43), recognizing that a similar mixed response by God's people was experienced in Isaiah's own day.

---

3. Walter C. Kaiser Jr. (with others), *Hard Sayings of the Bible* (Downers Grove: InterVarsity Press, 1996), pp. 126–127.

John 12:41 thus seeks to draw parallels about unbelief. Just as Isaiah could witness God's glory in the temple and be commissioned for witness to a stubborn generation (Isa. 6), so too were Jesus' signs and glory understood only by some. The overlap is not just illustrative, either: John includes the Son's glory in Isaiah's temple vision. The rejection of Jesus in the first century reflects past rejection of the triune God.

What we cannot conclude with any confidence is that the prophet saw Jesus' glory *exclusive of the Father's* or that Isaiah himself could have recognized and articulated this. There are several reasons for such caution.

In John, glory is never the Son's alone. The Father shares his own glory with the Son (e.g. 8:54; 13:31–32; 17:1–5). This is certainly an astounding claim, one echoed throughout the the New Testament (Heb. 1:3; 2 Cor. 4:6; Titus 2:13) so that the Father might be praised (Phil. 2:11; 1 Pet. 4:11; Jude 25). Thus it would be rather dissonant if John 12:41 were pressed to emphasize the Son's glory at the expense of the Father's. Once more we find the Son being *added* to the identity of God in the Old Testament and recognized in his activities. There's no sense in which the Son *supplants* other members of the Trinity in the process.

We should also be alert to the fact that the wording here does not add any clarity. John writes that Isaiah 'spoke about him'. We're not told how Isaiah understood and described Jesus. This is no clearer than Abraham's seeing Jesus' 'day', or other New Testament descriptions of the Old Testament being 'about' Jesus in some way. John's lack of specificity is further compounded when we realize he's not so much quoting Isaiah as paraphrasing him; there are lots of grammatical alterations between the two Bible passages. What we read in John is a summary and an interpretation in the light of John's own experience of Jesus. Just because John can identify the Son's glory as part and parcel of the Father's glory means neither that Isaiah could do this nor that it was the Son's glory alone that appeared in Isaiah 6.

At best, we might argue that John allows christophanies *as part of* theophanies. Seeing 'God' can be said to include seeing Jesus. We do not here find grounds for claiming christophanies *instead of* theophanies. An exclusive role for the Son needs to be established on other grounds, such as demonstrating the Father's compulsory invisibility or voluntary absence.

We can affirm this conclusion on other grounds. For a start, Isaiah's vision has often been interpreted as a sighting of the whole Trinity. This is traditionally based on the threefold 'holy, holy, holy' chanted by the seraphim (Isa. 6:3), though this repetition can be explained better in other ways. And if the New Testament is allowed to be uniformly definitive of Old Testament scenes – the very argument used by christophany proponents for taking John 12:41 as definitive of Isaiah's vision – there are good reasons to find either of the other members of the Trinity at work here. A corresponding throne-room scene in Revelation 4 records similar threefold praise of 'the Lord God Almighty': the one who sits on the throne and who is distinguished from 'the seven spirits of God' in front of the throne (Revelation's irregular way of describing the Holy Spirit) and from the resurrected Lamb (who approaches the throne in the next chapter, and who sits on the throne – along with, not in place of, the Father – only later in the story). Alternatively, we observe the words spoken in Isaiah 6 attributed to the Holy Spirit in the closing verses of Acts 28. Thus the same logic that thinks John 12:41 nominates the Son as the one seen on the throne in Isaiah 6 should lead us also (or instead) to identify the Father or the Spirit. The argument is thus handled wrongly by those who want to find here evidence of an exclusive christophany. Robert Reymond rightly allows that Isaiah 6 can be attributed to more than the Son, so elsewhere he claims too much when he uses John 12:41 to identify the Son exclusively.[4] Better, then, are those who understand that we must be careful about how definitive or restrictive we can allow New Testament passages to be. John Calvin was appropriately cautious in his understanding of Isaiah 6, despite being clearly sympathetic to the doctrine of the Son as the image of the invisible Father. He resolved, 'Yet, in my judgment, it is wrong to restrict this vision to the person of Christ, since the prophecy refers rather to

---

4. Robert L. Reymond, *A New Systematic Theology of the Christian Faith*, 2nd ed. (Nashville: Thomas Nelson, 2002), pp. 311, 313, 1099 versus pp. 158, 194.

God without any differentiation.'[5] Such caution can be traced back
at least as far as Theodore of Mopsuestia (AD 350–427):

> What did he [Isaiah] see? In the spiritual vision, in the revelation of
> divine nature, which is incomprehensible, Isaiah saw the glory that is
> common to the Father, the Son and the Holy Spirit, since Scripture
> cannot establish precisely whether it is the glory of the Son or the Holy
> Spirit. Therefore neither the Evangelist [in John 12] nor the apostle [in
> Acts 28] is in contradiction in saying that it is the glory of the Son or
> of the Holy Spirit.[6]

Modern commentators are increasingly coming to grips with
expressing the distinction between what Isaiah saw and knew and
the way in which John describes this in language appropriate to *John's*
audience and era. We may thus affirm the caution of Andrew Lincoln
when he concludes that 'In this case the thought is presumably that,
since Christ as the pre-existent Logos shared God's glory (cf. 1.1,
14; 17.5), all previous sightings of God's glory were also visions of
Christ's glory.'[7] This language does not rule out the possibility of
Old Testament christophanies. But it does recognize the two
emphases being pressed in the current analysis. First, any New
Testament descriptions of Old Testament events are not mechanic-
ally definitive of those events. Secondly, where the New Testament
intimates glimpses of Old Testament christophanies, these tend
towards christophanies *within* a broader sense of theophanies and
not *instead of* theophanies. God the Son may be identified in
these theophanies, but not at the expense of the other members of
the Trinity.

---

5. John Calvin, *Calvin: Commentaries*, LCC 23, tr. Joseph Haroutunian
   (Philadelphia: Westminster, 1958), p. 121.

6. Theodore of Mopsuestia, *Commentary on the Gospel of John*, tr. Marco
   Conti (Downers Grove: InterVarsity Press, 2010), p. 114.

7. Andrew T. Lincoln, *The Gospel According to St John*, BNTC (London:
   Continuum, 2005), p. 144; cf. Andreas J. Köstenberger, *John*, BECNT 4
   (Grand Rapids: Baker Academic, 2004), pp. 391–392.

1 Corinthians 10:4, 9

Very similar conclusions can be drawn for Paul's claims. He himself is clearly writing for a later audience and uses appropriately updated language for their benefit. Nor are his claims any more perspicuous than John's: they do not offer a detailed defence of or insight into Old Testament christophanies.

First, the Old Testament offers no verification of a moving, water-yielding rock in the wilderness. Paul is probably drawing on various Jewish traditions that built up around the ways God miraculously provided for his people in the desert. The tradition of a single rock that followed Israel derived from the mention of such a rock near the start and end of this forty-year period (Exod. 17; Num. 20).[8] If Paul is working from a tradition that developed beyond the pages of the Old Testament, how much should we let this tradition influence our reading of Scripture? The fact that Paul draws on material outside the Bible does not rule out the possibility of christophanies. But it does mean that, because the rock tradition cannot be verified from Old Testament texts, any reconstruction of Old Testament events must be uncertain. In particular, a closer reading of the biblical text in Exodus 17:6 shows that any promised manifestation of Yahweh is 'upon' or 'by' the rock, not 'as' that rock.

Secondly, once again we're dealing with a situation where Paul's contemporary language is describing some past event. We certainly cannot use Paul's description to reconstruct what the wilderness Israelites understood of any possible christophany.

Thirdly, it's not at all clear whether Paul's description in 1 Corinthians 10 is relevant to christophanies anyway. Definitions of christophanies commonly presuppose manifestations of God in human form. Christophanies are usually so humanlike that when God appears he cannot initially be distinguished from any other man. That is certainly the scenario painted persistently for the Angel

---

8. Among many studies in addition to commentaries, see e.g. Peter Enns, 'The "Moveable Well" in 1 Cor 10:4: An Extrabiblical Tradition in an Apostolic Text', *BBR* 6 (1996), pp. 23–38.

of the Lord – supposedly the regular form of christophanies. So James Borland is disappointingly inconsistent. His introduction concludes that 'The term *Christophany* in this work will denote those unsought, intermittent and temporary, visible and audible manifestations of God the Son in human form,' and that 'Christ alone appeared in the human-form theophanies.'[9] His subtitle reaffirms his focus on appearances *in Human Form*. So it flouts his own boundaries when he occasionally entertains non-human-form appearances such as the rock of 1 Corinthians 10:4, which, additionally, Paul implies followed Israel for a few decades longer than the average fleeting christophany.[10] Moreover, Paul expressly describes a '*spiritual* rock' from which came 'spiritual drink' as he parallels Israel's blessings with the blessings experienced by New Testament believers such as those at Corinth. Both the Israelite and Corinthian contexts are concerned with real food and drink as well as spiritual nourishment, but it seems an awkward stretch to move from 'spiritual rock' to 'tangible human-form theophany'. Yet that is precisely the inexplicable leap made by Charles Gieschen as he attempts to use 10:4 as '[t]he most substantive testimony' of the New Testament that the *Angel* accompanied Israel as a christophany. The same leap seems to be made subtly by Kaiser when he speaks of 'the one who *stood by* Moses' when he provided water.[11]

Fourthly, when Paul says that 'the rock was Christ', the word 'was' is no more definitive than we've found the word 'of' to be. The 'was' could of course equate the two directly. But it's telling that

---

9. James A. Borland, *Christ in the Old Testament: Old Testament Appearances of Christ in Human Form*, 2nd ed. (Fearn: Mentor, 1999), here his conclusion to pp. 13–17 and p. 59.

10. Ibid., p. 61.

11. Charles A. Gieschen, 'The Real Presence of the Son Before Christ: Revisiting an Old Approach to Old Testament Christology', *CTQ* 68 (2004), p. 117; Walter C. Kaiser Jr., *The Uses of the Old Testament in the New* (Chicago: Moody, 1985), p. 116 (my italics), echoed in his comments on 'Exodus', in *EBC*, vol. 1, p. 344. Kaiser is at least alert that this interpretation comes from 'Paul's view'.

Borland himself is elsewhere willing to tone down the connection and accept that 'the smitten rock *represented* Christ'.[12]

Fifthly, the mention of testing Christ in 10:9 provides no additional clarity. It does not tell us the Israelites recognized what they were doing. Again, as with the Angel of the Lord encounters with Gideon and Manoah, what a narrator can later describe is no guide to what the original participants grasped. Nor does Paul tell us that Christ is tested (by either the Israelites or the Corinthians) in isolation from God.

We thus reach the same conclusions as for John 12. The New Testament certainly affirms the Son's eternal existence and even his preincarnate activity. But any intimation of Christ's presence is in addition to and not in place of an any more general presence of God, and we certainly dare not suggest that Christ's distinct presence was known to the Old Testament generations.

The more usual explanation of 1 Corinthians 10:4 and other passages is far less novel. Paul is not *unmasking* Christ in the Old Testament. Rather, Paul *adds* the recently encountered second person of the Trinity to the identity of the Jewish God. The New Testament authors regularly ascribe the Old Testament titles and activities of God to Jesus as well. In 1 Corinthians 8:6 Paul expands the foundational 'one God' credo of Deuteronomy 6:4 to accommodate Jesus. In 1 Corinthians 10:4 he seems to allow that Israel's notion of God as their rock can be extended to (rather than replaced by) God the Son as well.[13] We have many examples where Paul makes this kind

---

12. James A. Borland, 'Exodus', in Edward E. Hindson and Woodrow Michael Kroll (eds.), *The KJV Bible Commentary* (Nashville: Thomas Nelson, 1994), p. 150 (my italics). The possible senses of 'was' are catalogued by commentators; e.g. Roy E. Ciampa and Brian S. Rosner, *The First Letter to the Corinthians*, PNTC (Grand Rapids: Eerdmans, 2010), p. 451.

13. Richard J. Bauckham, *Jesus and the God of Israel* (Milton Keynes: Paternoster, 2008), pp. 26–30, 97–104, 210–218; Bauckham's lengthy subtitle emphasizes *the New Testament's Christology of Divine Identity*. A classic study of applying the identity of God to Jesus is Murray J. Harris, *Jesus as God: The New Testament Use of Theos in Reference to Jesus* (Grand Rapids: Baker, 1992).

of accommodation: adding the New Testament Jesus to the Old Testament God, as it were. Despite the occasional claims and intricate hypotheses of scholars such as Hanson, we do not have examples of Paul's substituting Jesus in place of God.

As with John 12, we find that the simplistic methodology used for discovering Old Testament christophanies cannot be applied consistently. The methodology backfires and proves more than the Bible can bear, not unlike Frankenstein's monster rising to attack its creator. Consider the following scenario. Let's allow that Paul *is* developing Old Testament hints concerning the preincarnate activity of the Son, hints visible in the text. There's a rock that provides water for the wilderness generation in Exodus 17:6, distinct from Yahweh. The methodology used for finding christophanies would allow that here we have 'Yahweh' and 'rock' distinguished, just as in the New Testament God the Father and God the Son are distinguished. Note already that this is problematic, because here Yahweh (as much as the rock) sounds like he is making a visible appearance. When later Old Testament texts reflect on the wilderness events, they again distinguish 'God' = 'Yahweh' = 'the Most High' from the 'rock' through which he provided water (Ps. 78:17–22). Paul Blackham, arguably the British equivalent of James Borland with respect to christophanies, enthusiastically affirms this equation: 'the title "Most High" . . . is one of the most common Hebrew titles that is reserved for God the Father'.[14] The psalm even applies this title expressly when talking of testing God:

> they continued to sin against him,
>> rebelling in the wilderness against the Most High . . .

> they put God to the test
>> and rebelled against the Most High . . .
> (78:17, 56)

---

14. Paul Blackham, 'The Trinity in the Hebrew Scriptures', in Paul Louis Metzger (ed.), *Trinitarian Soundings in Systematic Theology* (Edinburgh: T & T Clark, 2005), e.g. pp. 39–40, 45–46.

So two more, interrelated problems arise. If the divine titles in the psalm are intentional – as Blackham insists they are throughout the Old Testament – then it's God *the Father* who is expressly tested. It's also difficult when the psalm elsewhere conflates the 'rock' and 'God Most High' (78:35). Christophany proponents cannot consistently apply both the claim that the various trinitarian identities can be carefully distinguished by the different divine titles and the methodology of allowing later texts to unequivocally clarify earlier ones. Later texts either identify the rock as God the Father or insist that it was the Father who was tested.[15]

So we ought to be circumspect about what we claim and the perspective from or for which we claim it. Craig Blomberg's summary of 1 Corinthians 10 demonstrates this safer balance:

> From a Christian perspective, Paul recognizes Christ as the pre-existent Son of God, active with God the Father in creation and redemption, and hence the agent of both physical and spiritual nourishment for his people in the desert.[16]

Jude 5

Those who champion christophanies confidently invoke Jude. The evidence will be viewed even more persuasively given that, since late 2012, authoritative editions of the Greek New Testament (designated NA[28] and UBS[5]) have reinstated 'Jesus' as the most likely subject of the verb. 'Jesus, who saved a people out of the land of Egypt, afterwards destroyed those who did not believe' (ESV).

Many scholars are reluctant to accept the word 'Jesus' here and think that whatever other term Jude wrote refers to Yahweh in

---

15. I explore Blackham's use of divine titles in 'Paul Blackham 2: Weak Theological Links', *Chm* 125 (2011), pp. 161–163.

16. Craig L. Blomberg, *1 Corinthians*, NIVAC (Grand Rapids: Zondervan, 1995), p. 191.

general or to God the Father in particular.[17] If they are right, the verse adds nothing at all to the quest for christophanies. However, accepting the more startling reading does not gain anything more than we've found from the other New Testament intimations of Jesus' preincarnate activity.

If Jude really mentions 'Jesus', we have no further idea what he means by this. There are no parallel passages to clarify how Jesus saved and judged his people (and, in the next verse, also wayward angels). It's quite reasonable to guess this could have been Jesus functioning as the Angel of the Lord, but that remains a guess and one that is only as strong as the arguments for that identification. The evidence is plausible but circumstantial. Moreover, it corresponds only to one of Jude's descriptions; one or more of God's angels (and not necessarily *the* Angel) contributes to leading the exodus generation, but there's no mention anywhere of angelic involvement in punishing their rebellion. The Greek sentence continues into Jude 7 (cf. ESV) but, despite frequent claims, a number of assumptions have to be made before we can link the Angel of the Lord with the demise of Sodom and Gomorrah.

At most, Jude appears to join the other early church leaders in confirming Jesus' involvement alongside God. There's no warrant here for singling out Jesus as if the rest of the Trinity were not participating.

The most we can say is that Jude is consistent with any christophanies that can be verified on other grounds. Jude in isolation offers no conclusive confirmation. We should certainly be cautious before developing any substantial theology or application from an uncertain word in an unclear verse. However admirable his aims, it seems to me such caution was carelessly abandoned by Blackham when he once preached the following:

> The great truth Jude wants us to grasp is that there were thousands upon
> thousands of ancient Israelites who were part of that great Church of

---

17. E.g. Douglas J. Moo, *2 Peter, Jude*, NIVAC (Grand Rapids: Zondervan, 1996), pp. 239–240; Thomas R. Schreiner, *1, 2 Peter, Jude*, NAC 37 (Nashville: B & H, 2003), pp. 444–445.

God in the wilderness, but they did not trust Jesus for themselves. They had deceived themselves. Although Jesus saved them from slavery and provided food and water for them in the desert, yet at the first opportunity they grumbled about Him and indulged in orgies and idol worship.[18]

Minor claims and assumptions

The other various claims should all be understood along the same lines. No one here doubts that God the Son has always existed and been active throughout history as part of the Trinity. What is in doubt is whether we should identify particular activities of the Son in Old Testament times and whether we can read any evidence of these in the pages of the Old Testament itself.

Many of the New Testament passages claim nothing more than the Son's eternal pre-existence. Pre-existence is, of course, necessary if there are to be Old Testament christophanies. But that claim does nothing to locate and demonstrate such appearances.

And we're persistently faced with the lack of precision that occurs when past (Old Testament) events are told in contemporary (New Testament) language. When Hebrews 11:26 speaks of Moses' willingness to endure 'disgrace for the sake of Christ', we can be certain only that this means something to the epistle's first-century audience. Despite the ends to which it's sometimes pressed, the phrase cannot validate what Moses himself understood. Moses valued something that can *now* be clarified as related to God's Messiah.

This is especially true of the passage in 1 Peter 1:10–12. There are many similar issues for which this passage is invoked, though not all relate to christophanies. Several more relevant matters need to be untangled.

First, authors sometimes get caught up in exactly what the Old Testament prophets were searching for. The consensus is increasingly that they were 'trying to find out the time and circumstances'

18. Paul Blackham, 'Contending for the Faith (Jude 1–7)', preached at
    All Souls Langham Place, London, 25 July 1999.

concerning the Messiah's sufferings and glories (1:11 NIV; cf. HCSB). This is in contrast to the suggestion that they were seeking 'what *person* or time' would be involved (ESV, NASB, NRSV). With the first term clarified, we're assured that the Spirit 'revealed to them, not *whose* sufferings they were about which they spoke – this they quite apparently already knew – but *when* the Messiah's sufferings were to occur'.[19] But note the misplaced confidence. Just because we're increasingly certain what the prophets *were* asking, we cannot use their silence to overspecify what else they might have known. On his preceding page, Reymond all but admits he is building his case on assumptions read into Peter's silence: 'he certainly does not say that they were ignorant of the Messiah's sufferings as such'. If anything, the passage is at pains to affirm that the prophets did not know everything!

Secondly, any descriptions Peter offers are relevant to *his* day, not the prophets'. His whole chapter is concerned with the faith and salvation that is for 'you', 'now', 'in the last time'. When Peter describes 'the Spirit of Christ' and 'the Messiah', he tells us only how first-century readers identified these individuals. It tells us nothing of the prophets' language. We can speculate about what the prophets grasped, but our insights remain secondhand and dependent on the words Peter uses to précis their quests. 'The effect of Peter's language is to emphasize not the secondary importance of the prophets' ministry, but the supreme importance of the future redemptive events to which they bore witness.'[20]

Thirdly, we can't even assume the order in which Peter came to this knowledge. He is certainly not repeating Old Testament passages that say clearly what he himself is summarizing. Rather, he gives

19. Reymond, *New Systematic Theology*, p. 523 (italics original); cf. Walter C. Kaiser Jr., 'Single Meaning, Unified Referents', in Kenneth Berding and Jonathan Lunde (eds.), *Three Views on the New Testament Use of the Old Testament* (Grand Rapids: Zondervan, 2008), p. 56.

20. J. Ramsey Michaels, *1 Peter*, WBC 49 (Waco: Word, 1988), p. 46; cf. Scot McKnight, *1 Peter*, NIVAC (Grand Rapids: Zondervan, 1996), p. 73.

every impression of revisiting the prophets in the light of his recent and startling experience of Jesus. This reminds us just how often we ourselves revisit the Old Testament sparked by some New Testament matter. If I might dare mention another contentious issue as a passing example: when Isaiah 7:14 foresees a 'young woman' (NRSV) bearing a son named Immanuel, there's nothing oddly supernatural envisaged. It's only when Matthew 1:18–23 cites this verse, and further clarifies that Mary conceived virginally, that we rethink what Isaiah understood and communicated.

Thus we dare not use 1 Peter to reconstruct the prophets' teaching in fine detail, especially where such teaching is not overtly present in the Old Testament. We're dealing here with the same 'retrospective' sense that has been the theme throughout part 3. One famous (American) commentator agrees with another famous (British) scholar in summarizing the implications:

> I. Howard Marshall is surely correct in saying: 'We do not need to envisage God as actually describing the Christian church to the prophets; it is sufficient that they were told that their prophecies would be fulfilled in the future "in those days and at that time" (Joel 3:1).' In other words, Peter is using Christian language (Spirit of Christ = Holy Spirit) to describe the experience of Old Testament prophets . . . Peter does not try, nor should we, to retroject the whole gospel into the mouths of the prophets.[21]

Peter's example actually alerts us to the fact that, if the New Testament is allowed to influence our understanding of the Old Testament, the New Testament may further teach *against* the possibility of Old Testament christophanies. I've touched on that spectre with passages such as John 12 and 1 Corinthians 10. We turn to consider a few additional texts.

----

21. Ben Witherington III, *Letters and Homilies for Hellenized Christians* (Downers Grove: InterVarsity Press; Nottingham: Inter-Varsity Press, 2007), vol. 2, pp. 83, 84, citing I. Howard Marshall, *1 Peter*, IVPNTC 17 (Downers Grove: InterVarsity Press; Leicester: Inter-Varsity Press, 1991), p. 46.

New Testament passages minimizing Old Testament christophanies

Our quest in part 3 is to demonstrate that readings of the New Testament that are too superficial can be irresponsible, not least when it comes to Old Testament christophanies. We can see the shortcomings of the methodology when we observe that the same process can be used to discredit the possibility of christophanies.

We've just considered 1 Peter 1. Scholars interested (for whatever reason) in Jesus' pre-existence note that the same chapter proceeds to mention how Christ 'was chosen before the creation of the world' (1:20). That verse concludes, 'but was revealed in these last times for your sake'. Although English presents only a 'but', the two halves are tied together closely in Greek. Further contrast is cemented by the two corresponding time phrases. We might formally represent the verse this way:

On the one hand,
  he was chosen
    before the creation of the world,

but on the other hand,
  he was revealed
    in these last times
      for your sake.

Peter is concerned to address his hearers 'in these last times' after Jesus' Easter ministry is completed. The surrounding verses expressly address Jesus' death (1:19) and his resurrection and ascension (1:21). And it's only now, in these last times, that 'he was revealed'. If we take these words as seriously as we're exhorted to take John 8:56, 12:41 and the like, Peter unambiguously implies that Jesus was *not* revealed previously. It cannot be objected that Peter means some special kind of enfleshed appearance; 'revealed' belongs to the same word group that simply means 'to appear visibly' (as in the very word 'christophany'). Peter says it was for this New Testament generation's sake that Jesus was finally revealed visibly.

Among several similar passages, we might consider Hebrews 9:26. Again in contrast with 'the creation of the world' we're told, 'But now He has appeared one time, at the end of the ages' (HCSB). We're assured that Jesus has become manifest only 'once', for his incarnate ministry. The word elsewhere in the letter is quite emphatic; the verses following confirm that humans are destined to die 'once' (9:27) and, as Protestants have long highlighted, Christ was sacrificed only 'once' (9:28). Some may protest that this 'one-time-only appearance' smacks of advertising hyperbole. It makes Jesus sound like a celebrity on tour. But the remainder of the paragraph confirms we've understood correctly. Jesus' first appearance, 'one time, at the end of the ages' (9:26 HCSB), is indeed one stop on an extremely limited touring schedule. Our author expressly counts the only other occasion, yet to be experienced, when 'he will appear a *second* time' at his final return (9:28).

(Speaking of celebrities and Hebrews, the letter's discussion of the enigmatic Melchizedek has sometimes been pressed as further evidence for Old Testament christophanies [7:1–10].[22] But modern christophany proponents and others are almost univocal in rejecting that possibility.[23])

Other passages not only praise the climax of Jesus' ministry during his incarnation, but suggest there has not been any comparable behaviour in the past. Acts 17:30 juxtaposes God's past tolerance of ignorant idolatry with his new command to repent. That is hard to reconcile with suggestions that Jesus had long been spreading the gospel through preincarnate appearances (and especially, if with those at n. 2 above, we're to accept that Old Testament saints such as Abraham were 'justified, like all

---

22. E.g. Hanson, *Jesus Christ*, pp. 65–72.

23. E.g. Borland, *Christ in the Old Testament*, pp. 139–147; Stephen, *Theophany*, p. 46; Ron Rhodes, *Christ Before the Manger* (Grand Rapids: Baker, 1992), pp. 247–248; David L. Allen, *Hebrews*, NAC 35 (Nashville: B & H, 2010), pp. 437–438; D. A. Carson, 'Getting Excited About Melchizedek (Psalm 110)', in D. A. Carson (ed.), *The Scriptures Testify About Me: Jesus and the Gospel in the Old Testament* (Wheaton: Crossway; Nottingham: Inter-Varsity Press, 2013), pp. 162–166.

Christians, through faith in Christ'). Paul closes his letter to the Romans praising God who entrusted Paul with his gospel, his new message that was a mystery for long ages but has now been revealed (Rom. 16:25). It's *now* revealed and made known through the prophetic writings' (16:26), intimating that the Old Testament was previously opaque in its gospel presentation. Indeed, the apostles sometimes clarify that saving faith – like Abraham's – is directed towards God the Father (Rom. 4:24; Col. 2:12; 1 Pet. 1:21) as much as the Son.

Other passages show that the broad array of arguments employed for identifying Old Testament christophanies simply cannot work as a collection. One or more of them must be altered or altogether abandoned. Consider Mark 12:26–27 (and parallels). The Sadducees confront Jesus and attempt to confound him with a question about resurrection. As part of his rejoinder, Jesus asks them what God said in Exodus 3:6. After citing the verse, Jesus again refers to God in the third person ('he'). We suddenly remember that the commissioning of Moses in Exodus 3:1–6 is a premier Angel of the Lord passage, with the preincarnate Son supposedly appearing to Moses. How, then, should we interpret Jesus' statements about 'God'? It seems to me that any of the three logical possibilities threatens to undo an interpretative 'rule' used to identify christophanies: (1) As we might usually assume, perhaps 'God' is how Jesus refers distinctly to the Father. If so, Jesus has expressly allowed that the Father *is* involved in visible theophanies. Moreover, he has expressly ruled the Son *out* of this key Angel passage. This would seem to forestall any further investigation of christophanies. (2) The language of 'God' is often broad enough to include Father and Son (and Spirit) and perhaps makes the best sense of Jesus' comments here. If so, we find yet more evidence that people, including Jesus himself, can refer to themselves in the third person. Christophany proponents must further relinquish the argument that the Angel, supposedly Jesus himself, is distinguished from God because of third-person references to God. (3) Perhaps in desperation someone might propose a more complex kind of theophany, as is sometimes suggested for Exodus 3. Perhaps the 'Angel' does the appearing while, separately, 'God' does the speaking. Christophany proponents must then relinquish any suggestion that different divine titles can be used to delineate different members of the Trinity. After all, in the same verse from which Jesus quotes we read that it's 'God' whom Moses is afraid to see; that should be a non-issue if 'God' refers to the invisible Father. And neither could anyone maintain that the Father is unheard; we have further grounds to challenge a superficial reading of John 5:37.

We noted earlier the problems that arise if we allow New Testament throne-room scenes to inform their Old Testament counterparts. There are various throne-room scenes in Revelation, and the Lamb at most shares the throne with his Father (esp. Rev. 3:21; 21:1, 3; perhaps 7:17). At all times the throne remains occupied by One who is distinctly not the Son/Lamb or Spirit (esp. 1:4; 4:2, 9–10; 5:1, 7, 13; 6:16; 7:9–10). Elsewhere Jesus himself refers to the throne of 'God' and the one sitting upon it (Matt. 23:22). The imagery of Hebrews is of the glorified Son seated beside 'the throne of the Majesty in heaven' (Heb. 8:1; cf. 1:3; 4:16; 10:12; 12:2). Stephen and Paul also report something approximating this (Acts 7:55–56; Eph. 1:20; Col. 3:1). The uniform message of the New Testament is that the heavenly throne is occupied by the one we would call God the Father. There's occasional mention of the Son's having a throne (Matt. 19:28; 25:31) but it pales in comparison with the consistent testimony of the enthroned Father. The interpretative rules that favour christophanies ought strongly to advocate that Old Testament throne-room scenes (most distinctly Isa. 6; though also the vision of 1 Kgs 22:19–23, the related imagery in Ezek. 1 and Exod. 24:9–11, and perhaps also Dan. 7) be explained in the light of this consistent New Testament reality!

I'm not thoroughly advocating every interpretation offered throughout this section. Each is included here principally to demonstrate that it can be inconclusive or counterproductive to allow superficial readings of the New Testament to resolve Old Testament enigmas. Such readings need to be handled more carefully than is usually done in the race to dazzle believers and unbelievers with the prospect of Old Testament christophanies.

That said, neither would any Christian reader dismiss the contribution of the New Testament. To the extent that the New Testament informs the Old, the momentum discovered here could equally argue that God the Son ventures into the world on his own only at the incarnation and that Old Testament theophanies are better interpreted as operations of God the Father or of the entire Trinity.

Additional factors

My case is complete for this chapter. Those interested in or committed to Old Testament christophanies may well want to explore further issues.

In addition to the factors already surveyed, I would suggest there are some helpful diagnostic questions when it comes to thinking about how the Old and New Testaments interact. This is a huge topic in itself, and we can scratch its surface only briefly. The following questions both offer some windows into the deeper complexities of the topic and provoke further thought.

Ordering?

In what 'order' do we approach the two testaments? Do we read the Bible from cover to cover like a novel, starting with God's initial revelation to Israel and then his fuller revelation to the church? Or do we begin at the end of the story and work backwards?

I've already used the idea of a detective story or mystery thriller. Do we claim to be reading the 'mystery' of the Old Testament for the first time, or are we rereading a favourite story knowing full well how it turns out?[24]

Directionality?

It's not a hermeneutical crime to revisit the Old Testament in the light of the New. It's precisely what many of the New Testament characters and authors have done. But it reminds us there's an 'order' in which Scripture unfolds. Further, it suggests that the 'directionality' of the connections is important. Moving from the Old Testament to the New cannot always be so easily reversed.

---

24. Peter Enns, 'Apostolic Hermeneutics and an Evangelical Doctrine of Scripture: Moving Beyond a Modernist Impasse', *WTJ* 65 (2003), pp. 276–277.

In considering precisely this issue in a book concerned with *Preaching Christ from the Old Testament*, Sidney Greidanus offers some helpful examples. Paul's allegory in Galatians 4 uses Hagar and Sarah for several illustrations, but we cannot use Genesis 21 to foretell Paul's points. Similarly, Matthew 1 compresses the genealogy of 1 Chronicles 3. We can see Matthew making a theological point, but we cannot derive this theology in advance from Chronicles.[25]

Circularity?

If there's both an order and direction between Old and New Testaments, the biggest danger is one of circularity. The diagnostic questions so far ask if we or others are reading the Old Testament responsibly. Have we confused first and subsequent readings? Have we projected forwards from the Old Testament a link that can be validated only with New Testament hindsight?

A useful statement on a related topic better balances issues of order and circularity: 'The Spirit's distinct personhood can, and according to the NT should, be read into the OT, but cannot be read out of it.'[26] That is, we can appreciate something of the Spirit's personhood in the light of the New Testament, but we cannot derive that personhood from the Old Testament on its own. Similarly, no one is suggesting God the Son has nothing to do with the Old Testament. It's just a question of how we should – and should not – be reading in and reading out.

Exclusivity?

Behind circularity is usually one more presupposition. A good many Bible readers presume that any New Testament adaptation of an Old Testament passage furnishes an *exclusive* and definitive interpretation.

It's all too easy to find otherwise good, godly scholars working with this interpretative model. They rightly recognize that clearer

---

25. Sidney Greidanus, *Preaching Christ from the Old Testament* (Grand Rapids: Eerdmans, 1999), e.g. pp. 189–191, 269.
26. J. I. Packer, 'Holy Spirit', in *NDT*, p. 316.

passages should influence our understanding of difficult ones. But they wrongly take the next step and decide there's only ever a *single* interpretation or application intended. This is especially the model employed by those favouring christophanies. Reymond instructs that 'Bible students . . . should strive to harmonize Scripture with Scripture because the Scriptures reflect the thought of a single divine mind.' Kaiser is likewise concerned to demand a one-to-one mapping between related passages.[27]

But we've repeatedly seen that one-to-one mapping is not the way in which every Old Testament passage is later used. The events and words of Isaiah's commissioning are attributed to both the Son and the Spirit. We can try to visualize both being involved, or we can recognize that the things of God can be variously *appropriated* in different ways without being exclusively definitive. Many other examples could be explored.

Those who would use New Testament texts to verify the events and identities of Old Testament passages must demonstrate that they have considered these factors of order, directionality, circularity and exclusivity. Yes, there are times when later texts can safely verify earlier passages. But there are many occasions on which we need to allow more flexible connections to occur.[28]

An example in practice

Walter Kaiser has been one prominent example of a scholar bringing 'christophany' language into circulation. As we move towards a summary of the New Testament's contribution, Kaiser himself illustrates important points from the current chapter.

God has graced Kaiser with a long and prolific writing ministry, and we often find earlier ideas refined later. Consider how Kaiser's

---

27. Reymond, *New Systematic Theology*, pp. 49–51, 103 (whence quote); Kaiser, e.g. 'Single Meaning, Unified Referents' and his other contributions to that volume.

28. See e.g. the contributions of Peter Enns and Darrell Bock to Berding and Lunde, *Three Views*.

expression concerning the Angel of the Lord has developed over three decades:

> To say that the patriarchs regarded Him as equivalent to a Christophany would probably be to claim too much. One thing for sure, He was not the invisible God. And He acted and talked as the Lord. There the matter apparently rested until revelation clarified the enigma.

> To say that the patriarchs regarded him as equivalent to *what the New Testament would call* a christophany would not be far from the truth. One thing for sure, he was not the invisible God. And he acted and talked as the Lord. There the matter apparently rested until revelation clarified the enigma later on, *when he was recognized* as a pre-incarnate appearance of Christ.[29]

Kaiser rightly acknowledges the influence of later knowledge and language in describing Old Testament events. But he then pushes too far in what he claims for the New Testament; nowhere does it 'recognize' the Angel of the Lord as an appearance of Jesus! Nor does it use 'christophany' either before or after Christ's incarnation.

Summarizing New Testament contributions

The way(s) the New Testament uses the Old is not a topic easy to explore or summarize. Whole books at popular and scholarly levels are devoted to it.

We should readily appreciate that later descriptions of earlier events are furnished in the idioms of the later context. My own discussion of Old and New Testament phenomena is occurring in English rather than Hebrew and Greek, and is accompanied by contemporary examples. Such modernized discussion should seem natural. We probably require our attention drawn to it before we notice what's happening.

---

29. Walter C. Kaiser Jr., respectively *Toward an Old Testament Theology* (Grand Rapids: Zondervan, 1978), p. 85; *The Promise-Plan of God* (Grand Rapids: Zondervan, 2008), p. 53 (my italics).

The same thing can be illustrated via an earlier example. Chapter 10 opened with N. T. Wright's discussion of the Queen. Even though he wrote these words more than a quarter of a century ago, most readers probably encounter the name 'N. T. Wright' and visualize the man who has *since* become a famous bishop and a prolific and sometimes controversial author. In what ways is it appropriate and inappropriate to retroject this contemporary image backwards to an earlier era?

What accommodation, then, do we make for New Testament descriptions of Old Testament events? I'm not by any means disavowing the relevance of either testament and I wholeheartedly agree with other conservatives that the two offer mutual interpretation. However, there are various and widely recognized disagreements over what constitutes 'mutual' and 'interpretation'. As I've tried to demonstrate throughout part 3, for me it's too simplistic to assume that any given New Testament statement must always clearly and exclusively determine the events and perceptions of Old Testament times.

When it comes to Old Testament christophanies, we find that the few New Testament texts that hint at the possibility are far from definitive. None of them clarifies a particular Old Testament passage (though John 12:41 comes closest). They certainly add weight to the orthodox doctrines of the Son's eternal pre-existence and his membership in the Trinity. But they do nothing more than add his name to or recognize his participation alongside the 'God' of the Old Testament. They don't single out the Son as the regular and exclusive divine person involved in theophanies. Christophanies must be verified on other grounds before the New Testament hints can be fully understood and bear any weight placed upon them.

Moreover, where christophanies are defined as visible manifestations, only the two comments in John mention anything being *seen*. Further, what is seen is not clearly the Son, but rather his 'day' or his 'glory'. The comments in 1 Corinthians 10 and Jude make no mention of the Son being visibly manifest let alone seen. These two latter passages (along with the two in John) can be employed only to make and defend the rarer claim that the Old Testament Israelites *recognized and responded to* the appearances exclusively of the Son in christophanies. Such claims are made and defended hazardously, precisely because there's no further evidence to work with.

The unclear and undefinitive New Testament summaries – made from a New Testament perspective using New Testament categories – ought not to be pressed to hypothesize that the preincarnate Son was comprehended by Old Testament individuals. Vague summaries on any topic can never be pressed as determinitive of what past figures actually grasped. We can readily summarize that Luke Skywalker was kissed several times by his sister and fought several duels with his father. We can rightly say that King George V fathered and raised King George VI. Though these summaries communicate succinctly and accurately sometime after the events, they cannot be definitive of what Luke Skywalker and George V actually knew at the time. Indeed, these particular summaries – accurate from our perspective and for our purposes – prove *false* with respect to what the original participants actually comprehended. (The Skywalker family tree surfaces only later. The elder George was neither 'King' nor 'V' when 'Albert' was born; and at best George could suspect his second son might one day reign, but could not be certain of either his succession or his throne name.)

We've also discovered a number of New Testament passages that appear to teach against Old Testament christophanies. To the extent that the New Testament is invoked as definitive, christophany proponents need to explain how such passages are to be interpreted: how they are to be accommodated within the framework being proposed.

Parts 1 and 2 have resolved that the mysteries of Old Testament theophanies may be better understood by not excluding a role for God the Father. The same applies here in part 3. This is not to insist that Old Testament language of 'God' applies only to the Father. It simply recognizes that some of the traditional New Testament passages thought to focus the spotlight exclusively on the Son allow equally well the participation of the Father and the Spirit throughout God's encounters with Old Testament figures.

12. WHAT CAN WE CONCLUDE ABOUT CHRISTOPHANIES AND THEOPHANIES?

One final illustration draws together several of the issues we've been considering. I trust you'll forgive that it comes once again from the widely known *Star Wars* saga. At the very least, this reinforces the observation from part 3 that ancient issues are regularly described by and illustrated with the contemporary language and idioms of the later audience being addressed.

The original movie only eventually came to be known as *Episode IV: A New Hope*. Enthusiastic cinema patrons in 1977 knew nothing of this subtitle or its enumeration within Episodes I–VI (and beyond). These additional episodes developed our knowledge of events a long time ago in a galaxy far, far away.

Creator George Lucas even had the luxury of rereleasing the original trilogy with various tweaks. Once he had finalized what the characters of Jabba the Hutt and Emperor Palpatine and Anakin Skywalker 'really' looked like, each was projected back into the former imprecise or incomplete presentations. Once it was feasible to comprehend better and represent better the major population centres like Mos Eisley and Cloud City and the 'bright center to the universe' (that we learn only later is called Coruscant), visualizations of each were enhanced or added. In the original movies, such people and places were either reasonable approximations, hinted at by name only, or were missing from the storyline altogether.

Purists argue over what constitutes the authentic experience. Do we show our children the older versions, so that their knowledge is expanded only incrementally, the way ours was? Or do we allow them to enjoy the updated editions, such that they experience a fuller and more integrated encounter with the *Star Wars* universe from their first taste? It's not always a straightforward decision.

The issues of christophanies

In many ways, finding christophanies in the Old Testament seems to me like an attempt to recut and rescreen an older storyline with the benefit of later insights and better special effects. Once we eventually discover what the triune God 'really' looks like, we start to project Father, Son and Spirit back into the earlier imprecise and incomplete presentations. Figures who were previously only reasonable approximations or hinted at by name or missing altogether are suddenly present and presented as if they had always appeared like this.

Purists again argue over what constitutes the authentic experience. Do we introduce unbelievers and believers to events only incrementally, as God first introduced himself? Or do we integrate the benefits of hindsight so that readers experience a fuller and more rounded introduction from their first taste? Again, it's not necessarily a straightforward decision.

Of course the parallels are not perfect. The stakes are much higher when it comes to understanding our triune God and his real universe. His foresight and direction are far superior to any human author's, and we ought not to suggest that God only eventually realized how things would turn out.

But the parallels are sufficient. For those preferring a different genre, we can equally well consider again a detective story or mystery thriller. Are we experiencing the unfolding adventure for the first time and gathering clues incrementally, or are we returning for a second or seventh reading knowing how things turn out?

It all depends on how much the author has known and incorporated in advance. Clever authors may indeed include various hints that we don't catch on our first pass. (Apparently, wise Hollywood directors are now intentionally and densely packing in so many useful allusions and background details that audiences are rewarded for watching more than once.)

God, the ultimate author of Scripture, certainly has the capacity to have included adequate hints throughout the story, whether we're thinking of the unfolding events of salvation history or the biblical accounts that record them. No one doubts his ability. The question is whether God *has* incorporated such hints.

I'm certainly not doubting that such hints exist on a variety of topics. The Old Testament is essential reading for New Testament Christians and for anyone interested in what Christians believe. It's of benefit to unbelievers and believers alike. When pressed to nominate favourites, I contend that Leviticus is one of the most gospel-focused books in the Bible.

I am, however, doubting whether christophanies have a role to play. It's not clear to me that such events took place in salvation history or that they have been recorded with any clarity in the Old or New Testaments.

Knowing Jesus in the Old Testament?

When people ask why I'm interested in the possibility of christophanies, I have two primary answers. Let's start with the second of these.

Some interpreters are so convinced by the possibility that they mandate that Old Testament faith looked barely different to New Testament faith. We've seen Anthony Hanson argue that 'Abraham saw Christ, and was justified, like all Christians, through faith in Christ.'[1] Walter Kaiser also writes concerning Old Testament salvation:

---

1. Anthony Tyrrell Hanson, *Jesus Christ in the Old Testament* (London: SPCK, 1965), p. 125.

But no less important was the fact that its *object* of hope was the coming
Son of God that New Testament believers have also been taught to
expect and to put their trust in. Indeed, salvation in the Old Testament
was part and parcel of the 'so great salvation' that stretched across two
testaments in a single unified approach as to how men and women
would inherit eternal life.[2]

The same sentiment is expressed strongly by Paul Blackham:

> Moses is an apostle of Jesus Christ – the gospel preached by Moses
> is exactly the same gospel preached by the New Testament apostles.
> The only point of difference is that Moses looked forward whereas
> the apostles looked back. The gospel has always been a matter of
> justification by faith alone in Christ alone since the beginning of the
> world . . . [T]he whole gospel of Jesus Christ is set out from the very
> first page of the Bible . . . So Scripture interprets itself in presenting
> to us the same message at all times and in all places.[3]

Although it's unclear whether one always drives the other, christophanies are regularly linked with concern for 'continuity in God's
soteriologic program'.[4]

When pressed, some of these authors allow that faith in 'Christ'
does not mean that Adam and Eve, Abraham and Moses could each
name the coming saviour as such. But their writings just as frequently

---

2. Walter C. Kaiser Jr., *Recovering the Unity of the Bible: One Continuous Story,
   Plan, and Purpose* (Grand Rapids: Zondervan, 2009), the concluding
   words of pp. 169–181 (ch. 13) on 'The Unity of the Bible and the
   Doctrine of Salvation in Both Testaments' (italics original).

3. Paul Blackham, 'Evangelicals and the Bible', in Iain Taylor (ed.),
   Not Evangelical Enough! The Gospel at the Centre (Carlisle: Paternoster,
   2003), p. 100.

4. E.g. James A. Borland, *Christ in the Old Testament*, 2nd ed. (Fearn:
   Mentor, 1999), pp. 62 (whence quote), 108–110; Robert L. Reymond,
   A New Systematic Theology of the Christian Faith, 2nd ed. (Nashville:
   Thomas Nelson, 2002), pp. 528–537; Charles A. Gieschen, 'The Real
   Presence of the Son Before Christ', *CTQ* 68 (2004), pp. 108–109.

fail to draw the careful distinction about updated labels that we've explored in part 3. Coupled with the zeal to demonstrate pre-incarnate appearances of the one who would come to be known as God the Son, modern readers can easily hear and interpolate a far more conscious faith being claimed for these Old Testament figures.

In turn, this issue of Old Testament salvation has a wide range of practical, pastoral and evangelistic applications. What we think about Abraham's salvation influences how we approach our and others' salvation. One huge debate over the last two or three decades, against which some of our authors (especially Kaiser) are reacting, concerns whether a person *must* recognize the person and work of Jesus Christ to be saved. It has been suggested that modern missions might be optional if it can be shown that Old Testament figures such as Rahab and Naaman – not to mention Abraham and Moses and David – were saved by God without a specific faith in Jesus; God could obviously still save people without such overt knowledge. Old Testament christophanies are one weapon recruited into the conservative arsenal to combat such inclusivism.

These applications are each important, whether on as small a scale as personal salvation or as broad a canvas as world mission. I'm not mounting a liberal challenge against any of these by raising a challenge against christophanies. I am suggesting, though, that such applications are better engaged without reliance on defences as weak as alleged christophanies.

Reading the Bible better

The more important of my two concerns with Old Testament christ-ophanies is that this notion proposes an interpretative framework that, in my opinion, can only mislead readers of the Old and New Testaments. Given that christophany proponents regularly promise that they are teaching a more accurate way to read Scripture, that claim should be tested. Where it's found wanting, I would hope they will be eager to embrace even more accurate options.

Although it should be no surprise, I'm frequently amazed at how much our own theological presuppositions shape how we read the Bible. I'm pleased that my thinking has been freshly kindled by Mike

Bird's textbook. For many of us, interpreting Scripture can be little more than trying to massage any given passage into our pre-existing models.[5] Those committed to a triune God will insist that Genesis 1:2 refers to 'the Spirit of God' at creation (so most versions) and baulk at 'a wind from God' (NRSV). They will further assume that this is the Holy Spirit in the full trinitarian sense that we know from the New Testament, without first thinking how the initial readers of Genesis might have perceived God's spirit. Those concerned to defend Jesus' virginal conception and the wonder of predictive prophecy will read Isaiah 7:14 as the surprise motherhood of a 'virgin' (so most versions) rather than of just a 'young woman' (GNB, NRSV, NET). A commitment to eternal security leads readers to explain differently the apparent warnings against falling away given in Hebrews. On such points, even conservative commentators can expend great energy trying to massage the text to match theology.

That sounds rather judgmental. Yet everyone does this. We just think it's right when we do it and wrong when someone else – usually some 'liberal' who does not 'really' understand the Bible or God – does exactly the same thing but with a distasteful outcome.

No doubt I too am guilty of the same approach. At various points, not least in part 1 with the New Testament passages about God's (in)visibility, I have explored interpretations that are not the most common. The question is whether such reconsiderations of the text yield more accuracy or less.

The responsibility of all readers is to work on these issues together. That does not entail that the text of the Bible means whatever we want it to mean, or that we choose whatever interpretation wins the majority vote this week. If that were the case, then any number of misinterpretations would still hold sway today, not least slavery of others unlike ourselves. Indeed, if the majority ruled, christophanies would be the staple of every Christian's diet. But it does mean that ideas like those I've presented in parts 1, 2 and 3 need to be in the public domain for scrutiny and wider discussion.

---

5. Cf. Michael F. Bird, *Evangelical Theology* (Grand Rapids: Zondervan, 2013), p. 199, citing J. Todd Billings, *The Word of God for the People of God* (Grand Rapids: Eerdmans, 2010), p. 5.

Where I've overlooked something important, I trust that others will (kindly!) correct the conversation. Where I've offered a new way of looking at things, I hope this may be taken on board and appropriated into theological frameworks.

I don't think I've proposed anything completely novel. Part 1 has shown how a number of theologians, past and present, have taken the time to think about God and his (in)visibility. It's only when a particular agenda, past or present, is served by God's utter invisibility that this presupposition is defended too hastily. Part 2 has explored how a new consensus of Old Testament interpreters is forming on the question of the Angel of the Lord. Although historical momentum means that there are still plenty of authors playing off Candidates 2 and 3 against each other, Candidate 1 is increasingly accepted among evangelical commentators. Part 3 has reminded us of the limits of contemporary language in reconstructing past events. There's no rocket science there either, though we don't always take the time or space to express exactly the difference between different eras' perceptions.

Nor should the ideas I've proposed be accepted uncritically. I don't want to sound convincing just because these words appear in print from a reputable publisher (or because you are partial to my choice of illustrations). You ought not even to be persuaded by some of the names I've added to footnotes. Rather, you should take others' ideas and mine and gauge how fairly they represent and integrate the various Bible passages that have been addressed. For Christian scholars and laity alike, Scripture is the final arbiter.

What then for christophanies?

Longstanding theological frameworks can be hard to modify or abandon. The momentum built up by our own personal, cultural and denominational traditions can be difficult to steer. And yet Christians' commitment to Scripture ought to leave us open to adjusting our course.

I've alluded occasionally to changing perceptions about slavery. And few Christians are unaware of the heated debate about the place of women in church leadership; regardless of one's position, it's clear that significant sections of many traditions are – in good conscience – deciding to revisit the wisdom that has been received to date. One further brief example illustrates the point that Scripture trumps long-received and orthodox-sounding presumptions if these can be shown to be imperfect.

For more than four hundred years Christians have delighted to believe that John's Gospel adds some exciting reasons for thinking of the Holy Spirit as a person. John records Jesus' referring to the Spirit as a personal 'he', even though this breaches correct Greek grammar (John 14:26; 15:26; 16:13–14). A veritable Who's Who of conservative authors have promulgated this fascinating discovery, with more recent and recognizable names including A. W. Pink, Martyn Lloyd-Jones, Charles Ryrie, Leon Morris, Michael Green, Michael Ramsey, Millard Erickson, Bruce Milne, J. I. Packer, D. A. Carson, John Frame and John Piper. The problem is that all these scholars have been looking at the wrong word or, as is often the case with christophanies, have simply repeated the argument that they have heard on the grapevine without exploring the possibilities and alternatives in adequate depth. The argument is treated too super-ficially because it yields the 'correct' answer.[6]

That's the tricky thing with christophanies. To orthodox ears they sound both plausible and attractive. But orthodox answers carry less weight if they are not demonstrated carefully. That is what I've been querying: How accurate are the arguments and evidence raised in their favour?

I'm certainly not convinced by what's been suggested to date. Again, this does not rule out the possibility that christophanies *are* an accurate reconstruction of Old Testament events and texts. That possibility, however, needs to be argued better along additional or different lines. We need to hear more concretely how the Father's strict invisibility applies to him alone and to sight alone. We need to

---

6. The arguments, counterarguments and proponents are catalogued by Andrew David Naselli and Philip R. Gons, 'Prooftexting the Personality of the Holy Spirit', *DBSJ* 16 (2011), pp. 65–89. They open their survey precisely by admitting, 'Sometimes well-intentioned people argue for the right thing the wrong way.'

discover clearer avenues for establishing a single Angel of the Lord figure who is demonstrably separate from the Lord himself. We need to be confident that the language reported in the New Testament bears some resemblance to the events, experience and language of the Old Testament. And we need to hear more about the evidence for distinct roles within the Trinity, with the Father and the Spirit *choosing* to abstain from physical and visible interactions with the world throughout Old Testament history.

Until that evidence is forthcoming, we need to be circumspect about what we claim for God's Old Testament interactions with his world. Christophanies can certainly be accommodated as part of that trinitarian activity, but the exclusive sense in which that word is increasingly employed is not yet convincing and is probably even unhelpful for Christian growth. I propose that it better honours the Trinity and the text of Scripture to allow that the Father and the Spirit are themselves involved in Old Testament theophanies. May both our theology and our exegesis be ever more enhanced, to the glory of God – Father, Son and Spirit.

INDEX OF SCRIPTURE REFERENCES

Particularly significant discussions are in **bold**.

For more information about IVP
and our publications visit

www.ivpbooks.com

Get regular updates at **ivpbooks.com/signup**
Find us on **facebook.com/ivpbooks**
Follow us on **twitter.com/ivpbookcentre**

Inter-Varsity Press, a company limited by guarantee registered in England and Wales, number 05202650. Registered
office IVP Bookcentre, Norton Street, Nottingham NG7 3HR, United Kingdom. Registered charity number 1105757.